THE FASTEST
CARS
FROM AROUND THE WORLD

THE FASTEST
CARS
FROM AROUND THE WORLD

MICHAEL BOWLER & JONATHAN WOOD

p

Page 2: Power personified, the muscular Lister Storm with supercharged 7-litre, Jaguar-based, V-12 engine and a claimed 200 mph on tap . . .

Page 3: The fabulous McLaren F1 LM, incorporating race-bred technology and capable of a stupendous 220 mph.

This is a Parragon Book
This edition published in 2000

Parragon
Queen Street House
4 Queen Street
Bath BA1 1HE, UK

Copyright © Parragon 1996

Designed, packaged and produced by
Stonecastle Graphics Limited

ISBN 0-75254-100-5

Printed in Italy

Photographic credits

All photographs by Neill Bruce Motoring Photolibrary with the exception of the following:
(Abbreviations: r = right, l = left, t = top, b = below)

The Peter Roberts Collection c/o Neill Bruce: pages 22-23, 26-27, 29, 30-31, 38, 41(t), 43(b), 44, 49(t), 56-57, 64, 68, 69, 75, 76, 77, 80-81(b), 84, 86-87, 88-89, 90-91, 92-93.
Andrew Morland: pages 50-51, 58-59, 60-61, 95(b).
McLaren Cars Ltd: pages 3, 72, 73(t).
Bengt Holm: page 11(b).
D. Hodges: page 95(t), 95(r).
Trevor Legate: page 8.
The National Motor Museum: pages 46-47.

With grateful thanks to Neill Bruce for his kind assistance and patience, and to the other photographers and copyright holders for their contributions.

Lister Storm photographed courtesy of Denbies Wine Estate, Dorking, Surrey, UK.

CONTENTS

INTRODUCTION

Man is a very competitive animal, and few pastimes evoke such instincts among otherwise staid individuals as does the challenge of fast cars; ever since the first engine-driven carriages chugged down a dusty track, the same old question has always been asked . . . *'What'll she do, mister?'* This book details just what the road-going production car is capable of achieving in the hands of independent testers with accurate instruments. Not optimistic statements by manufacturers, not exaggerated claims from keen owners reading inaccurate speedometers with a following wind, down a hill – but real timed speeds, as an average of runs in opposite directions.

The traditional method of showing who had the fastest car was to organise a motor race. The first officially timed event was the 732-mile round trip from Paris to Bordeaux and back in 1895 – Levassor won in a Panhard at 15 mph. The first land speed record was established by the Count de Chasseloup's Jeanteaud electric car in 1898 at 39.3 mph, eclipsed the next year by Jenatzy's electric Jamais Contente at 65.8 mph. The last record to be taken on a closed public road was in 1924 when Ernest Eldridge recorded 146 mph in the aero-engined Fiat at Arpajon, just south of Paris; and the first to break the 150 mph barrier was Malcolm Campbell with a Sunbeam, also aero-engined, in 1926.

By then, the ultimate speed records could only be taken by purpose-built machines, built either by enthusiastic amateurs or factory experimental departments. Now, 70 years on, such speeds can be attained by comfortable, fast road cars which have to provide so much more than just an impressive top speed figure; in fact, both BMW and Mercedes, have given up claiming top speeds and electronically restrict their cars to 250 km/h (155 mph) despite Germany providing the last stretches of unrestricted road in the western world – for those, we have assumed a simple 'chip-change' and calculated their real maxima.

All the cars chosen are standard road cars,

Ever since the arrival of the 911 over 30 years ago, Porsche have built fast cars; the data-base lists 22 different models that have exceeded 150 mph. This 1986 Carrera clocked 154 mph.

with the specifications as listed by their manufacturers. We have ignored any faster versions which have been prepared by special tuning companies, even when these are approved by the manufacturer. BMW approve of the work of Alpina and Schnitzer who run their touring car race-teams; Mercedes include some AMG-tuned cars in their own price-lists, and there are a number of German specialists who tune Porsche Turbos. From across the Atlantic, Callaway fits turbochargers to Corvettes; the Sledgehammer version has clocked 250 mph at Daytona Beach and it was driven there on the road.

It has always been possible to make a car go faster than the maker intended, but generally the car won't last as long and the manufacturer's warranty will be invalidated. If you want to work out how much faster a tuned car will go, a 10% power increase will give a 3.5% increase in ideal maximum speed provided the power peak has been moved to match the new top speed, or the gearing has been changed. If however, you increase the aerodynamic drag at the same time, by adding spoilers and wheel arches, you may increase stability but the maximum speed increase will be less than expected.

While maximum speed has long been used as an indication of general performance, it is

acceleration that drivers can legally use; actual driving conditions would suggest that the time taken to accelerate from 30-70 mph in an overtaking gear should be the most interesting, but few people carry such a comparison in their heads, so the time taken from 0-60 mph is generally used. Although this involves the sort of driving you shouldn't use on the road – clutch-dumping wheelspin starts – it is far easier to measure and compare 100% effort than anything less. In fact, the 0-60 mph time is very dependent on gear ratios as you lose a noticeable proportion of the overall time whenever you have to change gear; with these fast cars, a comparison of the 0-100 mph times is far more valid – gear change times and take-off techniques make less apparent difference.

While manufacturers will take such figures as part of comparison during development, there has been no world-wide standard that covers the last 40 years and some manufacturers have exaggerated more than others. Until the mid-'seventies they used to exaggerate power figures too – the American power race of the late 'fifties inflated figures well beyond those of their European counterparts. We can't go back to check what these should have been but, for performance figures, we have used those taken by independent magazines at the time. Not all magazines are as objective as each other. *Autocar* and *Motor* magazines, once separate then merged and latterly just *Autocar*, used professional recording equipment; drivers were trained to get the best out

of any car. In America, *Road & Track* and *Car & Driver* have been equally objective. The vast majority of the figures here have come from these sources; where other magazines' figures have been borrowed, these have only been used after careful checking of test methods and confirmation by calculation. To all of them I am grateful for the use of their hard work; I spent many hours doing the same myself in the 'sixties at the Motor Industry Research Association track.

Nowadays, *Autocar* and other British magazines use the General Motors facility at Millbrook near Luton. While a lap round the banked track is accurate up to 150 mph, speed is scrubbed off by cornering beyond this, so some of the cars listed in the 150-175 mph bracket may be able to go 2-3 mph faster – certainly none of them is exaggerated. Faster cars will have been tested in Germany or at the high-speed Italian track in Nardo, or at American equivalents.

The Database lists 150 different production models that have reached at least 150 mph; naturally there are a large number from Ferrari and Porsche. From these we have selected 43 that have exceeded 160 mph regardless of age; but within the chapters most of the others have been mentioned as part of the development story that has led to the fastest, and usually latest, equivalent model. Some of those that have still to confirm their ability have been included in the final chapter.

'What'll she do, mister?' – Now you know.

'This book details just what the road-going production car is capable of achieving in the hands of independent testers with accurate instruments.'

Jaguar have a strong competition record but mostly just build cars that are comfortable and quick. This XJ220 was a statement that Jaguar technology is still up with the best of them; at 217 mph only two are faster.

AC COBRA 427

1965
160 mph
(257 km/h)

Few cars have captured the imagination of the performance world as the Cobra did in the mid-'sixties, and the legend has lived on through the many replicas to emerge again in the Viper, its spiritual successor. It was the time-honoured recipe of getting the biggest possible engine into the lightest frame that could handle the power and clothing it in an attractive two-seater body, preferably an open top for maximum enjoyment on the open road.

While the AC marque was founded back in 1901, the Cobra story starts with the 1953 introduction of the second generation Ace. Engineer John Tojeiro had created his own sports two seater modelled on the Ferrari 166 Barchetta (little boat); Tojeiro's cars were powered by MG or Bristol. He sold the design to AC who installed their own 85 bhp 2-litre six-cylinder engine; in

Carroll Shelby added muscles to the AC Ace, first with the 4.7-litre Ford V-8, then as the Cobra with the 7-litre Ford in a new, stronger chassis. The competition Cobra shown was originally raced by John Woolf.

1957, a Bristol 2-litre version was introduced giving another 30 bhp and a maximum around 115 mph.

A Ford 2.6-litre version followed in 1961 with anything from 100-170 bhp.

All was to change in 1962 when Carroll Shelby, impressed by the performance of the AC-Bristols in American racing, persuaded AC to drop a Ford V-8 into the spacious engine compartment. Fitting the initial 260 cu.in. (4.2-litre) lightweight engine was little problem but the suspension and drive-train needed considerable beefing up to take double the previous power output. AC were soon turning out five engine-less cars a week for Shelby to install Ford's engines and gearboxes; the 4.2-litre would soon be replaced by the 271 bhp 4.7-litre (289 cu.in.).

Not content with a mere 270-350 bhp from the small block Ford, Shelby wanted even more power, so the 7-litre Ford (427 cu.in.) was inserted, but only after the chassis had been given the Ford computer treatment. The main chassis tubes were increased in diameter to 4-inches, the car was widened and the old transverse leaf springs were

replaced with proper wishbones and coil springs all round; the chassis was adopted for the subsequent 4.7-litre versions from 1964. It was these uprated 289s using a mixture of open and coupé bodies that gave the Cobra its World Sports Car championship victory in 1965; there weren't enough 427s built for them to race in International GT racing but they were successful in American SCCA events.

On the road they were everything that they set out to be, fast and fun but somewhat lacking in creature comforts. Although the 'fifties ACs were appropriate for the time, by the 'sixties they were feeling dated alongside more sophisticated designs like the Lotus Elan. The 289 was the pleasanter road car; with narrower tyres it was lighter to drive and didn't twitch on every white line; but it was still shatteringly fast off the line reaching 100 mph in 13.7 seconds for *Motor* magazine. *Motor* also tested a competition version of the 7-litre with 580 bhp which could reach 100 mph in under 10 seconds, accompanied by raucous bellowing from the twin side exhausts. Noise and the sheer exhilaration of the performance were abiding memories of both cars, and the shape had a timeless beauty.

Finding true performance figures for the two models is difficult as magazines seem to have tested them in a variety of different states of tune and a choice of axle ratios. American tests of the original 260 version claimed 100 mph in 10.8 seconds which was faster than many managed with the later 427; it was always difficult balancing the wheelspin for the best times. Reasonable figures for the later, wider 289 would suggest a maximum of 145 mph with the later 3.31 axle, 0-60 mph in 5.2 sec and 0-100 mph in 13.0 sec.

The standard output for the 427 was 425 bhp, but they could also be bought in Street/Competition form with 485 bhp. *Motor* magazine tried the latter and recorded 0-100 mph in 10.1 seconds, which was very fast indeed for 1965. Others observed a maximum speed of 160 mph which corresponded to a heady 7000 rpm. The Cobras were real muscle cars.

SPECIFICATION	AC COBRA 427
ENGINE	V-8 6998 cc (427 cu.in)
HORSEPOWER	485 bhp @ 6500 rpm
TRANSMISSION	Manual 4-speed
CHASSIS	Twin tube steel
BRAKES	Discs all round
TOP SPEED	160 mph (257 km/h)
ACCELERATION	**0-60 mph** 4.6 seconds **0-100 mph** 10.1 seconds

'On the road they were everything that they set out to be, fast and fun.'

ASTON MARTIN V-8 VANTAGE

1977
170 mph
(274 km/h)

'It was a much more comfortable car than its predecessors.'

With 375 bhp, Newport Pagnell's bespoke Vantage was the world's fastest four-seater in 1977.

Big but still elegant, the V-8 Vantage put Aston Martin firmly into the 'seventies supercar league and gave the company a justifiable claim as producers of the world's fastest four-seater production car. Motor racing in the 'fifties and James Bond in the 'sixties had put Aston Martin on the world map as the car you promised yourself, one day. The V-8 Vantage made sure that its performance would be in keeping with its reputation when that day arrived.

In days when most supercars weighed no more than a ton and a half, the 4000 lb Vantage needed a pretty impressive power output to keep up. The trusty 5.34-litre four-cam V-8 was worked on to produce a reliable and tractable 375 bhp thanks to four big downdraught 48 IDF Weber carburetters, bigger inlets valves and a better exhaust system; with a drag factor of 0.38, this enabled a maximum speed of 170 mph; but, even the standard V8 saloon had 300 bhp which was good for nearly 150 mph.

While James Bond had made the DB series famous – he used a 147 mph 1963 DB5 – and these continued through to the DB6 Mk II, Aston's then owner David Brown wanted to produce a genuine 4-seater which even the longer wheelbase DB6 didn't really achieve, and it had to be faster than the 4-litre cars. Accordingly work started in 1963 on a new all aluminium V-8 engine. While the new car might have been one designed by the Italian coachbuilder Touring, who had styled the DB4, the company switched to one designed in-house by William Towns; although the extra width of the V-8 engine demanded a new chassis, this was essentially just a widened DB6 with new bodywork, but there was an important change in the rear suspension which adopted a de Dion axle.

Unfortunately development on the V-8 wasn't as fast as with the rest of the car, so the new DBS had to start life in 1967 with the 6-cylinder 4-litre engine; it was a much more comfortable car than its predecessors, but inevitably it was slower. It was

1969 before the V-8 was finally ready with 315 bhp using Bosch fuel injection to give a top speed of 160 mph. That the 1977 V-8 produced less horsepower was a function of increasingly restrictive emission laws.

Between the 1969 launch of the DBS V-8 and the 1977 170 mph test, Aston Martin went through two changes of ownership and a six-month shut-down. Sir David Brown had, for a long time, run Astons at a loss, almost as the promotional arm of the David Brown Corporation; by the end of 1971 this had to come to an end and Company Developments took over the ownership, and successfully continued development of the renamed Aston Martin V-8. By the end of 1974, they were in trouble and had to put the company into receivership; although the service department continued, production stopped. New owners, American Peter Sprague and Canadian George Minden, started in July 1975, to be joined six months later by Alan Curtis. Enthusiasts all, they soon had the V-8 back in production and started development of the new razor-edge Lagonda, also styled by William Towns. The intention had been that a new Aston shape would follow as a two-door version, but that never happened. Everyone was quite happy with

the old V-8 style; in 1978 this was further revised with an integrated tail spoiler, a result of the Vantage development which had reduced the drag.

With steady refinement, the Vantage was to stay in production for another 12 years from the date of this test; even now it is still a very quick car.

Filling in the grille area and allowing engine air to enter through the spoiler usefully lowered the drag factor, opposite: Middle East cars retained the V-8 grille for extra cooling.

Almost as fast were the limited run of Vantage Volantes; obvious Vantage details were supplemented by wheel arch flares and sill mouldings.

SPECIFICATION	ASTON MARTIN V-8 VANTAGE
ENGINE	Aluminium V-8 four-cam, 5340 cc
POWER	375 bhp @ 6000 rpm
TRANSMISSION	Manual 5-speed ZF
CHASSIS	Steel with aluminium body
BRAKES	Discs all round
TOP SPEED	170 mph (274 km/h)
ACCELERATION	**0-60 mph** 5.4 seconds **0-100 mph** 13.0 seconds

ASTON MARTIN VANTAGE ZAGATO

1986

186 mph

(299 km/h)

'It was to be the renewal of an old association which brought Aston Martin back, once again, among the world's fastest cars.'

Back in 1984, Aston Martin needed a new model. The same shape had been in production since 1967 when it was launched with the 6-cylinder engine, but a completely new model was too expensive. A new suit of clothes would be more affordable.

It was to be the renewal of an old association which brought Aston Martin back, once again, among the world's fastest cars. Back in 1959, the company wanted to produce a special lightweight version of the DB4GT; they went to the Italian styling house of Zagato in Milan and 19 models were built from 1962-4. Twenty-five years on, the new owners were looking for a similar extension to the Vantage range at the time of the 1984 Geneva Motor Show; they visited the Zagato stand. Founder Ugo Zagato had died, but the company was being run by his two sons, Dr. Elio and Ing. Gianni.

During the earlier Aston Zagato production, the Italian company was building a number of niche models for the various separate Italian manufacturers. By 1984, the major part of the Italian industry was controlled by Fiat and Zagato needed to find work outside Italy. The arrival of the Aston principals, Victor Gauntlett and Peter Livanos, was manna from heaven. Shortly after that motor show meeting, the general specification for a new Zagato-bodied Aston Martin was agreed – light enough to reach 60 mph in under 5 seconds and aerodynamic enough to achieve 300 km/h with 435 bhp, with just two seats and a probable production of 50 cars.

The engine to be used was the trusty V-8 which had been the company's mainstay from 1969. An aluminium 5.3-litre unit, it had twin overhead camshafts for each bank with four downdraught Weber carburetters sitting in the vee.

With 50 examples built, the 1986 Zagato-bodied Aston was more successful if less appealing than the 1961 DB4GT Zagato. Bonnet bulge, less obtrusive than prototype version, hides downdraught Weber carburetters.

As used in the V-8 saloon and Lagonda it developed around 300 bhp, and 375 bhp for the Vantage; a more powerful 435 bhp version was developed for the after market with bigger carburetters, new camshafts, higher compression and larger exhaust manifolds and this was the one fitted to the Vantage Zagato.

The Zagatos set to work and would probably have had a prototype ready for the following Geneva show had Aston Martin not imposed a 6-month delay in the middle. As it was, there was only a sketch for show visitors, but this and the Aston Martin and Zagato reputations were enough to persuade 50 buyers to place deposits over the next six months.

Finally, three prototypes were at the 1986 Geneva Show, and production of the 50 cars began shortly afterwards. Aston Martin sent a rolling chassis out to Italy, a working platform which had already been tested on the road. Zagato built a new superstructure, fitted the aluminium panels, trimmed the interior, painted the car and then sent it back to Newport Pagnell. Despite mixed feelings about the styling, there was no doubt about its appeal or its performance.

The car that was offered to the press was one of the prototypes and the French magazine *Sport Auto* was the only one to record a true maximum speed. Using a piece of unopened motorway, they achieved 299 km/h, only 1 km/h short of the target. The 0-60 mph figure came to 4.8 seconds – on target.

That prototype had a somewhat unsightly power bulge on its bonnet to clear the downdraught carburation. Originally, it had been intended to fit fuel injection to the Vantage engine, as had been developed for the less powerful V-8, but this was never completed on the two-valve engine; however Zagato designed the bonnet around the lower profile of an injection system and had to change this after the overall shape was finalised. The prototype's bulge was roughly shaped at the factory; although Zagato designed a much less obtrusive bulge for the production cars, the press never forgot and always drew attention to that bulge. How it should have looked was seen on the subsequent Volante Zagato convertibles, a limited run of 35 cars fitted with the less powerful injection engine.

Awesome in its noise and performance, the Vantage Zagato served its purpose and put Aston Martin back into the supercar league.

After the Vantage Zagato came 35 Volante Zagatos, here showing how flat the earlier bonnet would have been with fuel injection.

SPECIFICATION	ASTON MARTIN VANTAGE ZAGATO
ENGINE	Aluminium V-8 four-cam, 5340 cc
POWER	435 bhp @ 6000 rpm
TRANSMISSION	Manual 5-speed ZF
CHASSIS	Steel with aluminium body
BRAKES	Discs all round
TOP SPEED	186 mph (299 km/h)
ACCELERATION	**0-60 mph** 4.8 seconds **0-100 mph** 11.3 seconds

ASTON MARTIN VANTAGE

1993
184 mph
(296 km/h)

'But the handling is all that you expect and want from a powerful rear-wheel-drive sports car.'

Understated it is not. The latest Aston Vantage is a far more brutal version of the standard car than any Vantage has ever been since the name was coined for the DB2's more powerful engine back in 1951. Then and through the DB series, Vantage just meant more power; it wasn't until 1977 that Vantage became a separate model, recognisable at a glance with wider wheels with wheel-arch flares and a wind-cheating front with fashionable and effective front air-dam.

The standard Virage isn't slow with a maximum speed around 157 mph, but it has a fair amount of weight to get under way, so the 0-60 mph time is not really to Aston standards – at 6.8 seconds, it is slower than a Volkswagen Corrado VR6. And the Virage is designed for comfortable fast touring, so it lacks the handling tautness that the traditional Aston driver expects. The Vantage addresses these relative shortcomings in full measure.

The standard engine is a development of the original Marek-designed aluminium V-8, only it now has four-valve heads designed by the American Reeves Callaway, who had been responsible for the race engines used in the 1989 AMR-1 race programme.

In full emission form this develops 335 bhp. For some time, the traditional way of increasing power has been to use turbo-charging, but this brings with it the problem of turbo-lag – the delay in response to the throttle while the turbos build up speed; big turbos for big engines take even longer, which is why the Bugatti uses no fewer than four units. Aston Martin decided to revert to the 'thirties traditions of supercharging, where the units are directly driven by the engine and thus provide instant response; the drawback is that this consumes extra power so fuel consumption suffers. Using twin Eaton 'blowers' the 5.34-litre V-8 now produces a massive 550 bhp, but still has tremendous torque –

550 lb.ft. is more than any other production engine.

The traditional ZF 5-speed gearbox has been replaced by a 6-speed version used in the Chevrolet Corvette; five gears are used to power the Vantage up to its maximum speed with sixth an overdrive, giving a very long-legged 42 mph per 1000 rpm. *Autocar* testing saw 177 mph in fifth gear around the Millbrook bowl and there was more to come; Aston Martin say the car has recorded 191 mph, so we have settled for an average of the two at 184 mph at a red-lined 6500 rpm, which is the point at which the engine develops its maximum power. In acceleration, the new Vantage is very quick despite weighing nearly two tons; 0-60 mph in 4.6 seconds and 0-100 mph in 10.1 seconds put it into the top ten, and it is the only four-seater among them.

Heavy fuel consumption – you might get 15 mpg – is one drawback, but there are others

SPECIFICATION	ASTON MARTIN VANTAGE
ENGINE	Supercharged aluminium V-8 5340 cc
POWER	550 bhp @ 6500 rpm
TRANSMISSION	Manual 6-speed
CHASSIS	Steel with aluminium bodywork
BRAKES	Discs all round with ABS
TOP SPEED	184 mph (296 km/h)
ACCELERATION	**0-60 mph** 4.6 seconds **0-100 mph** 10.1 seconds

inevitable when you try to make that size of car handle like a two-seater sports car. The suspension has been considerably stiffened to keep roll angles down, so the ride is bouncy while wide low profile tyres add to the road noise that this generates; and the engine is far from quiet until you drop into that long-legged sixth. But the handling is all that you expect and want from a powerful rear-wheel-drive sports car; the front responds well to the steering and the back answers to the throttle.

The standard Virage was launched in the winter of 1988 after a very quick design period. The original V-8 was costly to build and many of its parts, borrowed from other manufacturers, were long obsolete; Virage thinking went back 10 years when a new V-8 was planned as a shortened version of the more modern Lagonda, only this would have its own body. The first Virage prototype was a shortened Lagonda to test all the mechanical components; and the new body came from the RCA duo, John Heffernan and Ken Greenley, echoing the past in a new modern shape. The Vantage took Astons back into the supercar league.

Steroidal Virage has 550 bhp thanks to twin super-charged V-8 with muscular bulges to match. Interior trim is to legendary Aston levels with full instrumentation.

ASTON MARTIN DB7

1994

161 mph

259 km/h

'Aston's own tests produced 165 mph.'

A convertible DB7, that was accorded the marque's traditional Volante name, appeared in 1996. Its top speed of 155 mph is slightly less than that of the coupé.

After a gap of 24 years, the DB7 has continued the range of numbers that David Brown set up when he took over the company in 1947. As Sir David Brown he had sold the company at the end of 1971 when the DBS was in production; the six-cylinder DB6 Mk II had stopped in November 1970. However Sir David was brought back into the fold as patron when new owners, Ford, started the design of the new small Aston; he was delighted to allow the use of his initials for the new car – in fact, the original DBS was nearly called a DB7.

Throughout the 'eighties, Aston's previous owners, Victor Gauntlett and Peter Livanos, had recognised that the company needed an entry level Aston 2+2 to join the Porsche 928 and Mercedes SL market. Unfortunately there just wasn't sufficient capital available to be able to embark upon the design and production of an entirely new car; to be possible it would have to borrow a number of parts from an existing higher-volume manufacturer. When Ford took over in 1987 this began to look possible, but it wasn't until Ford absorbed Jaguar in 1989, that the possibility moved to the probable; a combination of Ford engineering know-how and a Jaguar base would provide the appropriate background. While Jaguar had supplied some components for Aston Martin V-8 and Lagonda models, they weren't keen to provide too much until Ford came along to define the markets for the two former rival marques more precisely.

Jaguar had long intended to replace the XJS with the new XJ41 once the XJ40 – the 1986 XJ6 – was in production; to many this was regarded as the F-type successor to the legendary E-type. A number of XJ41 prototypes had been built when it was decided that the production cost would be too high for the numbers that could be sold as Jaguars; in a bid to rationalise the situation, Jaguar then put

the new XJ41 body design onto the existing XJS platform as Project XX. Ford axed this one too, but it was to provide an excellent basis for a small Aston Martin which could be priced at a more realistic level for lower volumes. Work started on the Aston version – Project NPX – in 1991.

Jaguar componentry offered a number of advantages, not least a well developed platform with independent rear suspension. There was also the six-cylinder Jaguar AJ-6 engine which would form a logical progression from the DB2-6 range, provided it could be Astonised. This was achieved by taking an unique 3.2-litre version of the AJ-6 engine and adding a supercharger to give 335 bhp

to match the Mercedes 500SL V-8 at 320 bhp and the Porsche 928 S4 at 350 bhp. Closed circuit tests showed a maximum of 157 mph, but Aston's own tests produced 165 mph, so our quoted figure is a mean of the two.

Jaguar had, of course, continued to develop the latest XJ6 which was launched in October 1994 as an evolution of the previous model. One derivative has been the XJR, a sports saloon using a 4-litre AJ-16 development of the AJ-6, also with an Eaton supercharger; this has been tuned to produce slightly less power than the Aston's at 321 bhp, but with slightly more torque. The result is a 155 mph full four-seater only marginally less accelerative than the DB7 but £33,000 cheaper.

But the proof of the pudding is in the eating. Forgetting the mixed heritage, the new Aston does provide exactly what was required for a little sister to the Virage range, and in time it will spawn its own Vantage and convertible versions. Designed to match the DB6 in length, it is lower and wider with a body style that is evocative of its predecessors, despite that 24-year gap. It looks and behaves just as one would expect an Aston to be.

The lines of the DB6 are discernible in the 7, a tribute to stylist Ian Callam. Like its predecessor, power comes from a twin overhead camshaft, six-cylinder engine although the DB7's is supercharged. Bumpers are present but concealed beneath deformable front and rear panels.

Left: The DB7 uses the traditional ingredients of walnut veneer and leather although the combination did not feature on the earlier cars. It is the work of Neil Simpson, like Callam, a Royal College of Art graduate.

SPECIFICATION	ASTON MARTIN DB7
ENGINE	Supercharged straight-6, 3239 cc
POWER	335 bhp @ 5600 rpm
TRANSMISSION	Manual 5-speed
CHASSIS	Steel with some composite panels
BRAKES	Discs all round with ABS
TOP SPEED	162 mph (259 km/h)
ACCELERATION	**0-60 mph** 5.8 seconds **0-100 mph** 14.4 seconds

BMW M1

1979

162 mph

261 km/h

A combination of German components, Italian styling and (initially) engineering, the mid-engined, glass-fibre-bodied M1 with its miniature radiator grille was unmistakably a BMW. Created to break Porsche's dominance on the race tracks, production delays rendered this impossible. This is a 1980 road car, one of some 400 built that were required to homologate the racing versions.

Undeniably sleek and sporting, the Giugiaro-designed M1 is thus far unique in BMW history for its mid-engined layout; the six-cylinder 3.5-litre 277 bhp unit, featuring twin overhead camshafts and four valves per cylinder, sits in line behind the cockpit, driving the rear wheels through a ZF transaxle.

Its purpose was to take part in the Group 4 and Group 5 categories of International sports car racing, where Porsche had dominated with the competition 911 Turbo, the 934 and 935. For this, at least 400 examples had to be produced over a 2-year period; in competition tune the M1 engine could be made to produce 470 bhp, so it had a theoretical chance against the 934, and the mid-engined layout gave it potentially better roadholding. The turbocharged versions, with up to 850 bhp, could challenge for outright victory.

Although Giugiaro drew up the M1's shape, its origins were firmly based in the 'experimental safety vehicle' Turbo concept car that BMW displayed to celebrate the Munich Olympics in

1972; designed by BMW's Paul Bracq, this incorporated side impact bars in its gull-wing doors and soft end panels mounted on rams among many safety features, but it was the mid-engined layout that was of particular interest. The power unit was the, then familiar, four-cylinder 2-litre, mounted transversely and fitted with a turbocharger to give around 200 bhp; it was this engine that was fitted to the 2002 turbo the following year, albeit de-tuned to 170 bhp. Only two of the concept cars were built, but they gave BMW the chance to assess mid-engined handling advantages, and provided styling cues when it came to the M1; the black belt-line and the low slender nose – later to appear in similar form on the 850 – were obvious carry-overs for Giugiaro to adopt.

With the decision taken in late 1976 to produce the M1, BMW contracted Lamborghini to do the design, development and production build of the new car; low volume production of such a car wasn't possible within BMW, and Lamborghini were looking for outside work. And

Giugiaro wasn't far away to keep an eye on the lines. Design and development during 1977 went well, but Lamborghini then had financial problems and couldn't undertake the production. Eventually in late 1978, production commenced as a joint exercise between Giugiaro and Bauer in Stuttgart. Giugiaro's ItalDesign company didn't have production space, but he sub-contracted the build of the tubular chassis and glass-fibre bodywork, mated the two and trimmed the interior. Bauer installed the mechanical components and completed the trim; thus it wasn't until 1980 that the required 400 were built, by which time the racing rules were set to change for 1982 and they didn't suit the M1 which was too heavy for the new formula.

Meanwhile BMW launched the Procar series for 1979; M1s in 470 bhp form had their own

races at *Grands Prix* with GP drivers like Nikki Lauda at the helm. It certainly gave the M1 instant acclaim and justified another 50 or so racing versions being built. They had some success in other races, but the loss of those two years meant that the M1 never had the chance to tackle the Porsches seriously in Group 4 racing or the faster Group 5.

Despite the fact that it couldn't achieve what it set out to do, the M1 was a superb 160 mph road car in the supercar mould and it played a useful part in promoting BMW's high performance image. It looked the part, it was well built with luxurious trim; it was a good cross between Italian design flair and German production engineering .

The M1 looks good from any angle. The long rear deck was necessary to accommodate the longitudinally-mounted ,3.5-litre, twin cam six, located ahead of a five-speed ZF transaxle.

The M1 was only produced in left-hand drive form and its interior borrowed components from across the BMW range. Despite this the cockpit could not relate to any other model. The speedometer reads to 280 km/h (174 mph).

SPECIFICATION	BMW M1
ENGINE	6-cylinder, 3453 cc
HORSEPOWER	277 bhp @ 6500 rpm
TRANSMISSION	Manual 5-speed
CHASSIS	Steel frame, glass-fibre body
BRAKES	Discs all round
TOP SPEED	162 mph
ACCELERATION	**0-60 mph** 5.4 seconds **0-100 mph** 13.5 seconds

'Giugiaro wasn't far away to keep an eye on the lines.'

BMW 850CSi

1994
170 mph
274 km/h

Coupés have been an intrinsic part of the BMW family for many years. The existing range is no exception and the 8 Series is stylistically outstanding and goes as well as it looks. This is a 1995 V-12 powered 850CSi although at the time of writing (1997) only the V-8 engined version is offered.

The German factory has a long history of producing high-speed coupés. In the 'thirties, the construction of the autobahns encouraged manufacturers to create ever faster cars; the BMW 327/80 was an elegant streamlined coupé that would reach over 90 mph on its 80 bhp and its design was carried over to become the post-war Bristol 400 with a style that was still modern ten years later.

In the 'fifties BMW were struggling for an identity, making big V-8 powered saloons and little motorcycle powered Isettas with nothing in between. The 507 was the two-seater sports coupé, using the running gear of the bigger saloons in a somewhat different style, the traditional twin intakes on a horizontal plane – very much a period classic.

Came the 1961 resurgence of BMW with the launch of the new generation heralded by the 4-door 1500 and the Munich firm embarked on the line that is recognisably still with us – clean, modern lines characterised by the ever-present twin radiator intakes in a variety of proportions, and always classically front-engined rear-drive. The basic single overhead camshaft engine configuration was unchanged for many years, but all except the smallest 4-cylinder engines now have twin camshaft four-valve heads. The first coupé in this range was the 2000C in 1966, the top of the range at that time.

When the 6-cylinder engine arrived for larger cars in 1968, the 2800CS came too, slightly shorter and with two doors. This became the 3.0CS in 1971 and on into the competition 3.0CSL – the

SPECIFICATION	BMW 850CSi
ENGINE	Aluminium V-12 5576 cc
HORSEPOWER	380 bhp @ 5300 rpm
TRANSMISSION	Manual 6-speed
CHASSIS	Unitary steel
BRAKES	Discs all round with ABS
TOP SPEED	170 mph
ACCELERATION	**0-60 mph** 6.5 seconds **0-100 mph** 15.4 seconds

Left: The underbonnet view is equally impressive with the twin overhead cam V-12 filling the entire engine compartment. It was originally produced in 5-litre form and then enlarged to 5.6-litres in 1993. A six-speed manual, or four-speed auto gearbox is fitted.

same, only lighter, with some aluminium body panels. By 1975 BMW had embarked on the new model designations, a type number preceding the engine size, as 525 – 5-series with 2.5-litre engine. From then on, the coupés have had their own series and more distinctive styling to set them apart from their saloon cousins; the first was the 630CS in 1976, a range enlarged two years later with a new cylinder block for the 635CSi, its 218 bhp making it a 140 mph car. When BMW introduced the M range, the 1983 M635CSi had a twin overhead camshaft 4-valve engine to give 286 bhp and over 150 mph, still a very desirable car 12 years on.

The coupés were always the top of the range and were produced in smaller numbers but, by using many body panels from the saloon series, they were not too much more expensive; the 6-series used a 7-series front end and running gear, and continued to use the old parts when the new 7-series arrived in 1986; part of this new range was the 750i using a 5-litre V-12 with 300 bhp which could obviously outperform the 635CSi, which was also looking a bit dated.

So to get the coupé back on top of the range, BMW created the 850i using the same magnificent V-12 in a style that stood well apart from the other models, still a beautiful car several years after its 1989 launch. The late 'eighties was the heyday of the very fast cars and it was appropriate that BMW should have one capable of 160 mph. Greener thoughts brought in a smaller engine, the all-new 4-valve 4-litre V-8 with 286 bhp which was

added to the 7-series range in 1992. This lighter, more efficient unit made the cars almost as fast as those with the V-12, so a 5.6-litre 850CSi version was added with 380 bhp, and the 850Ci was enlarged to 5.3-litres and 326 bhp; those who wanted the looks and less power could have the 286 bhp 840Ci which was added to the range at the beginning of 1993.

Performance figures taken on the 300 bhp 850i produced a maximum speed of 159 mph. Although BMW now limit the maximum to 155 mph, another 27% of power should certainly yield 170 mph, so the acceleration figures below have also been adjusted. Some have described the 8-series as anachronistic, a car with only style, even more performance and less space to separate it from the 7-series; but it is a superb style.

'The late 'eighties was the heyday of the very fast cars.'

It goes without saying that comfort is the keynote of the 850CSi. This is enhanced by the fact that the seats and steering wheel can be adjusted to suit the driver's requirement and this information is retained electronically. The 'wheel also moves out of position to permit easy entry.

BMW M5

1994
170 mph
274 km/h

In 1972, the year that Munich was host to the Olympic Games, BMW founded their subsidiary, BMW Motorsport GmbH. While the two-door 2002 series and the four-door saloons had been raced with great success by private entrants using tuning conversions from Alpina and Schnitzer, rule changes demanded that any special competition parts be available in specified quantities, which could really only be made by a manufacturer.

So BMW had to get involved if the cars were to continue racing, even if the tuners ran the actual race teams. Setting up a competition department, separated from the production factory, was common practice among the companies that had works entries in International events. The long hours required didn't upset the factory unions and it was also a sure way for lessons learnt in racing to be transferred back to the factory engineers.

The mid-'seventies was a good period for touring car racing in Europe and America; BMW had their share of success with the 3.0CSLs against the Ford Capris, and special versions even took on the Porsches. BMW were also to the fore in Formula 2 racing. By the end of the decade, touring car interest was waning and BMW wanted to join Porsche in GT racing, so the Motorsport department arranged to produce the mid-engined M1 (see separate story) in 1978; that it wasn't a racing success wasn't the fault of BMW – the rules had changed again, so they joined the *Grand Prix* world instead, using a turbocharged version of the original 4-cylinder BMW engine with the Brabham team, netting a 1983 championship with

Understated wolf, the M5's six-cylinder engine is stretched to 3.8-litres and tuned to 340 bhp – more than the 4-litre V-8 540i – and will reach 170 mph.

Nelson Piquet. Although there were subsequent *Grand Prix* victories in this 1000 bhp turbocharged era, BMW withdrew from Formula 1 at the end of 1986, by which time the name of BMW M-power was well established.

By now the Motorsport division's name was being used for high performance versions of regular road cars, the first to bear the name being the 1983 M635 CSi which used the four-valve engine that had been developed for the M1; with a later fuel injection system, this had 286 bhp. When the new 5-series saloon came along in 1984, this same engine was put into the top version early the next year to create the M5, the first time that BMW used this new model system.

SPECIFICATION	BMW M5
ENGINE	6-cylinder, 3795 cc
HORSEPOWER	340 bhp @ 6900 rpm
TRANSMISSION	Manual 6-speed
CHASSIS	Unitary steel
BRAKES	Discs all round with ABS
TOP SPEED	170 mph
ACCELERATION	**0-60 mph** 5.4 seconds **0-100 mph** 13.6 seconds

The 2-door 3-series had been introduced in 1982, but the M3 appeared after the M5. This used the four-cylinder engine as a 2.3-litre with four-valve heads to develop 200 bhp. While M-power was the point of the exercise, the cars had to be completely reworked as they were handling more than double the power of the base models – wider wheels, firmer suspension, bigger brakes and aerodynamic appendages combined to produce sports car behaviour in family saloons.

While the M5 was just a fast road car, the M3 was the basis of a very effective touring car racer and won many championships; it has continued to do so with the latest 162 mph M3 following its mid-1992 launch – now with a 286 bhp 3-litre six-cylinder engine. The new 5-series came in 1988, the latest M5 equipped with a 3.5-litre six with 315 bhp; this was enlarged to 3.8-litres in 1992 with 340 bhp and given a sixth gear and even lower profile tyres in 1994. It was in this final form that it clocked 170 mph, albeit in its 5th gear as 6th is very much a cruising overdrive.

The M-series have produced some remarkable cars and they are not just racing saloons; you can have the same specifications for an M3 convertible or the M5 estate car.

There is little outward evidence of the changes wrought by the Motorsport division; bigger wheels, deeper spoiler and a little M on the tail hide a comprehensive rework of suspension and engine.

'It was in this final form that it clocked 170 mph.'

BUGATTI EB110

1993

218 mph

351 km/h

'It may not be everyone's idea of beauty, but it is undeniably dramatic.'

Parked neatly on the Bugatti stand at the 1995 Geneva Show were three examples of the EB110, each proclaiming a world record. The EB110 Supersport laid claim to being the fastest production car with a maximum speed of 351 km/h (218 mph) which was achieved during its official ministry testing at the Nardo test-track in southern Italy; the McLaren has clocked 231 mph there but not as an officially observed run. The second record was for the fastest car using methane gas as a fuel – 344.7 km/h (214.2 mph). And the third was the fastest speed ever recorded on ice – 296.3 km/h (184.1 mph) achieved on a stretch of frozen sea somewhere in the arctic circle region. Impressive. However you look at it, the Bugatti EB110 is a very fast car of exceptional stability.

The Bugatti name has a long history with a big break in the middle before its recent restart. Italian-born Ettore Bugatti set up his factory in Molsheim in 1909; over the next thirty years he produced a selection of delectable motor cars for competition and road use. Sometimes they were advanced, latterly they were technically dated, but they always had style whether they were purely for racing – like the GP types 35, 51 and 59 – or such road cars as the glorious Royale or the design pinnacle of the type 57 on which son Jean Bugatti created such wonderful forms. After World War II, with Ettore's health failing, the company struggled to regain its former glories, but failed; it was finally taken over by Messier, the last real Bugatti having emerged in 1952. While there were several attempts to revive the name with the *Grand Prix* type 251 in 1956 and a sports car in 1960, the name passed into history for nearly 30 years.

Its revival has been due to a consortium of businessmen led by Romano Artioli, with Bugatti's son Michel (by his second marriage) on the board as the family connection. In 1988, a new factory

Ettore Bugatti was born in 1881; the new Bugatti was launched 110 years later, an engineering jewel with a shrink-wrapped skin.

was set up in Italy at Campogalliano near Modena, supercar land inhabited also by Ferrari and Lamborghini. The first car would be the EB110, announced in 1991, 110 years after the birth of Ettore, and it would be a technical masterpiece worthy of the best of Bugatti.

The new car embodied all that was state of the art at the time. The carbon fibre chassis was built by Aerospatiale; the racing-style suspension was developed by Messier Bugatti, specialists in aircraft undercarriages; transmission was provided to all four wheels through a six-speed gearbox adjacent to the mid-engine; and the engine itself is a 60-valve V-12 3.5-litre (then the *Grand Prix* size) with four small turbochargers to deliver an impressive 550 bhp at 8000 rpm. Aerodynamic control comes from underbody venturis and a tail wing that rises on stilts.

The style of its aluminium bodywork – the material of true craftsmen – is attributed to Lamborghini shaper Marcello Gandini with adjustments by Benedini. It may not be everyone's idea of beauty, but it is undeniably dramatic and contains some original Bugatti styling cues like the little horseshoe intake set within the grille. Following its extravagant series of launches in September 1991 in Paris and Molsheim, it moved into slow production. It is now available in two forms, the EB110GT with 550 bhp, and the EB110S with a massive 611 bhp at 8250 rpm; despite all that technology under its skin it weighs just 1600Kg. Small wonder, then, that it is very

fast; one magazine has recorded a 0-60 mph time under 4 seconds; *Road & Track* and *Autocar* recorded 4.5, with the former recording a maximum speed of 213 mph on a shorter straight than Nardo's banked track.

The EB110 is certainly a technical masterpiece. Those who have built such supercars can only marvel at how such a technology showcase can be produced for under £300,000 when every part has been designed from a clean sheet of paper.

SPECIFICATION	BUGATTI EB110S
ENGINE	Quad-turbo V-12 3499 cc
HORSEPOWER	611 bhp @ 8250 rpm
TRANSMISSION	Manual 6-speed with 4WD
CHASSIS	Carbon fibre with aluminium body
BRAKES	Discs all round with ABS
TOP SPEED	218 mph
ACCELERATION	**0-60 mph** 4.3 seconds **0-100 mph** 9.2 seconds

CHEVROLET CORVETTE

1996
170 mph
273 km/h

'The result is an almost completely new car.'

A '97 Corvette, with headlamps ablaze, that is wider and longer than its predecessor and is also improved aerodynamically. Brakes are excellent, a combination of big discs and calipers and wide tyres. As previously, it is only available in left-hand drive form.

Chevrolet's seemingly evergreen Corvette sports car was radically revised for the 1997 season and this fifth generation model looks all set for a long production run. It is also noticeably faster than its predecessor that in stock form had a top speed nudging 160 mph. The new car is capable of 170 mph and is accordingly quicker off the mark.

The 'Vette has been around since 1953. Created by General Motors in response to the British sports cars that were finding favour among young Americans, the original version was powered by Chevrolet's six-cylinder 3.8-litre engine and was capable of a rather unpredictable 100 mph. The open two-seater roadster body was made of glass-fibre and this material has been a feature of the Corvette ever since.

The original six was replaced by a V-8 engine, of 4.3 litres, in 1955 and all versions have thereafter been so equipped. Top speed was approaching 120 mph.

In 1962 the Corvette was greatly enhanced by the appearance of a new body, the work of GM's newly appointed styling supremo, William Mitchell. The assured lines of what was allotted

the Sting Ray name betrayed a strong European influence and the open car was joined, from the outset, by a coupé version. Mechanical refinements included the creation of a new chassis and introduction of independent rear suspension.

By the time the car ceased production in 1967 it was available with a choice of V-8 engines, with a top of the range 7-litre unit capable of endowing the model with a flat-out speed of 135 mph.

The next Corvette of 1967, which arrived at the time of the Muscle Car era in America, perpetuated the top line V-8 with no less than 560 bhp on tap. This David Holls-styled car, the Stingray name spelled as one word and revived in 1969, was capable of 160 mph in its most powerful guise and endured until 1982.

By this time the roadster version had been discontinued in 1975, and from thereafter only coupés with a Targa-style roof were built. Its successor of 1983 was destined for a record 13-year production life and incorporated a hatchback. The backbone chassis was new and there was a birdcage tubular structure to which the glass-fibre panels were bonded. To European eyes, the all-independent suspension was curious in that the

medium utilised was glass-fibre transverse leaf springs. At the front this was used in conjunction with wishbones although at the rear the driveshaft served as an upper link.

Although this 5.7-litre model was a 160 mph car, 1989 saw the arrival of a potent variant, the 180 mph ZR-1, with aluminium rather than cast iron V-8, a 32 valve engine developed by in-house Lotus. The mainstream model also benefited, in 1991, from a new power unit, the 5.7-litre V-8 replacing an original that dated back to 1955.

The current car was announced late in 1996 for the 1997 season. It has been a long time a-coming, work on the project having begun in 1990, only to be jeopardised when Chevrolet's cash strapped parent, General Motors, nearly axed the model.

But the glass-fibre-bodied Corvette, with its long established lineage, survived and the result is an almost completely new car, although one that is visually related to its predecessor.

The two-seater coupé, with a similar detachable Targa-style hardtop, has been stylistically and aerodynamically refined so that it possesses a drag coefficient of 0.29 which is one of the lowest in the business. Its reliance on a simple but well proportioned shape with a minimum of external decoration, suggests that it is intended for a long manufacturing run.

The new car is wider and longer and, although the front mounted V-8 engine retains the same 5.7-litre capacity, dimensions and pushrod activated valves of its predecessor, it is a new design with an alloy block rather than a cast iron one and develops 345 bhp, as opposed to 300.

A further departure from previous practice is the introduction of a rear-mounted, Borg-Warner

six-speed manual gearbox although a four-speed automatic is an optional offering.

The tubular steel perimeter chassis is also new which GM claims is four-and-a-half times stronger, and 36 kg lighter, than the frame it replaces.

The transverse-leaf, independent double-wishbone suspension – a combination that had hitherto been exclusive to the front – has been extended to the rear.

A further innovative feature is the fitment of Goodyear Extended Mobility Tyres. These EMT covers are so called because they can run flat for up to 200 miles and obviate the need to carry a spare wheel, so saving valuable boot space and weight. An indicator on the dashboard immediately registers any drop in tyre pressure.

The 'Vette feels very much like its predecessor although with a strong emphasis on refinement. This is a much more comfortable car and suspension can be set according to road conditions, namely Tour, Sport and Performance, while the claimed 0-60 mph figure of 4.7 seconds is 2.3 seconds faster.

Nowadays the Corvette has competition from the home grown Dodge Viper, the Japanese and the Europeans in the form of the Porsche Boxster and BMW Z3. But if past experience is anything to go by, this version should run and run . . .

Left: Like all its predecessors, the current 'Vette is glass-fibre bodied. The circular rear lights have been a feature of the model since 1961. The ducts in the front wings have been designed to allow hot air to escape from the brakes.

SPECIFICATION	CHEVROLET CORVETTE
ENGINE	Aluminium 4-cam V-8, 5680 cc
HORSEPOWER	345 bhp @ 5600 rpm
TRANSMISSION	Manual 6-speed
CHASSIS	Steel perimeter
BRAKES	Discs all round with ABS
TOP SPEED	170 mph (273 km/h)
ACCELERATION	**0-60 mph** 4.7 seconds **0-100 mph** 13.3 seconds

The last Corvette roadster was built in 1975 and since then it has only been made with a Targa-style detachable roof. The latest version is no exception and the car in the foreground has its roof panel detached. This is stowed in the big boot, there being no spare wheel, made possible by the use of run-flat tyres.

CHRYSLER VIPER VENOM

1995
187 mph
301 km/h

The Dodge Viper is marketed in Britain under the name of its Chrysler parent although without right-hand drive and this is the original version of 1993 vintage. Selling for £55,000, it had stupendous, if raucous, performance and a top speed of 167 mph. The brakes were accordingly large but, by all accounts, fade free.

The Viper sets out to be an anachronism and even more so in its 550 bhp Venom form. It has been created around the old-fashioned concept of enjoyable open motoring, raw fun on four wheels. But there it is, in the maximum speed table, up amongst the finest examples of supercar engineering, the Venom proving usefully quicker than the standard car and particularly with its hard top. Old fashioned it may look, but there is some new technology under that skin.

There are other cars with some of the same retro appeal, like the TVR Griffith, but the Viper has more in common with a 1965 Shelby Cobra than with Blackpool's best. What sets it apart from this decade is the big lazy engine – an 8-litre V-10 – and the studied lack of creature comforts; you didn't expect a quiet ride in a Cobra, or a snug-fitting roof, but you did expect raucous high performance in any gear, just like the Viper. Against the Cobra it is 7 inches wider and 5 inches lower, a Cobra with a modern stance.

The common denominator is indeed Carroll Shelby – Shelby who put Ford V-8s into AC's very British sports car and won a World Championship, the same Shelby who then worked over Chrysler saloons to transform their performance. And Shelby has been in the background of the Viper development. But the concept was Chrysler's, spurred on by President Bob Lutz, an arch enthusiast for the sheer fun of driving anything that challenges the driver.

The Viper was first shown as an eye catcher on the Dodge stand at the 1989 Detroit Motor Show, a fully-engineered eye-catcher that was there to gauge public reaction to retro-styling in general and the Viper in particular. Either way it was well received and, three years later, it reappeared ready for production which can reach up to 5000 units a year should the demand be there.

Its chassis is built up in sheet steel stiffened by large box-sections in the sills and central tunnel, and substantial bulkheads each side of the cockpit.

The Viper GTS is the coupé version, better equipped and its performance enhanced by the use of aerodynamic aids. Created as a one-off in 1993, it entered production in 1996 and its body and engine are lighter than the roadster's.

'The body is 'sixties curvaceous but made from a modern acrylic plastic.'

All independent suspension uses double wishbones at each corner, and the steering is power assisted; it needs to be with that big engine weight coupled with massive tyres – the front wheels are ten inches wide and the rears thirteen. The grip generated is prodigious.

That front-mounted engine started life as a cast-iron truck unit, but has been re-engineered with aluminium block and heads by Lamborghini, who were owned by Chrysler at the time. The standard Viper 7990 cc V-10 develops 406 bhp and the Venom version gets 550 bhp thanks to straightforward head, manifold and cam improvements. Even the Venom unit has a low specific output, so both versions should last. Mated to them is a six-speed Borg Warner gearbox with an axle ratio giving such high gearing that it only needs 1400 rpm to cruise at 70 mph in sixth. The most sophisticated part of the car is the engine/transmission management system which controls the fuel injection and also inserts a detent to prevent selection of second and third gears when accelerating gently, thereby saving fuel during emission testing.

The body is 'sixties curvaceous but made from a modern acrylic plastic. The overall style follows the rounded sports car themes of Mazda MX-5 and Suzuki Cappuccino, but the squat proportions and the sheer size make it a very impressive beast. And standard Viper performance is a match for its ancestor; the 7-litre Cobra, too, would achieve over 160 mph given the right

SPECIFICATION	CHRYSLER VIPER VENOM
ENGINE	Aluminium V-10, 7990 cc
HORSEPOWER	550 bhp @ 6000 rpm
TRANSMISSION	Manual 6-speed
CHASSIS	Steel with acrylic panels
BRAKES	Discs all round
TOP SPEED	187 mph (301 km/h)
ACCELERATION	**0-60 mph** 4.4 seconds **0-100 mph** 9.7 seconds

gearing and reach 100 mph in around 10 seconds. The Venom is usefully faster. But the charm of both is the ability to accelerate so quickly in any gear; accompanied by an explosive roar, you can blast past anything in whatever gear you happen to be. It is an exhilarating but tiring drive, a big toy built for driving pleasure rather than practical commuting.

The more potent Venom 600 of 1997 with 635 bhp on tap. Like the mainstream model it uses a Targa-type roof although the no-frills Viper is an uncompromising two-seater with the anti rollover bar just ahead of the rear window surround.

DE TOMASO PANTERA GT5-S

1986
160 mph
257 km/h

'The 200 denotes 200 mph, but no one has yet put this to the test.'

While the original shape Pantera is the fastest recorded, this Gandini-restyled version should be faster still in its twin turbo form.

After early forays into building single-seaters for Formula Junior and Formula 2, Alejandro de Tomaso joined the ranks of Italian sports car builders back in 1963.

The first offering was the mid-engined Vallelunga which used a backbone chassis to which was bolted a 1600 cc Ford Cortina engine; this took all the rear suspension loads via arms on the transaxle bell-housing. The theme was extended at the 1965 Turin Show with a sports-racing car using a bigger backbone which carried a 271 bhp Ford Mustang engine; never raced, this formed the basis of the Mangusta using body styling by Giugiaro while he was working at Ghia. Production started in 1967, the year that de Tomaso acquired Ghia – Ghia built the bodies in Turin and de Tomaso fitted the power train in Modena. The same year saw Ghia in production with the Giugiaro-designed Maserati Ghibli.

Meanwhile, Ford of America, having tried to buy Ferrari in the early 'sixties, were still on the look-out for an Italian supercar to add to the Lincoln range. They liked the Ghibli and came to look at the Mangusta in 1969, at which time Tom Tjaada had just completed a scale model of a new Ford-powered sports car. Ford didn't like the Mangusta, largely because it wouldn't pass the forthcoming stricter American safety standards, but they saw a better future for the Tjaada car and

signed an agreement in September 1969 for technical cooperation between Ford of America, Ghia and de Tomaso who would build concept cars and niche vehicles for Ford. The first of these would be the Pantera, to be built at the rate of 10,000 a year with de Tomaso retaining the right to non-American sales.

Dallara came from Lamborghini to redesign the chassis which followed contemporary racing practice with a sheet steel monocoque centre section with strong sills; Ford's latest 351 cu.in (5752 cc) V-8 was attached to the rear and mated to a ZF transaxle. Ghia didn't have enough space to assemble the cars in the required quantity so de Tomaso acquired the Vignale factory in late 1969. Less than a year later, Ford had acquired 84% of de Tomaso's Ghia/Vignale/Pantera operation.

Nearly 300 Panteras were sold in Europe in 1970, but American approval didn't come until 1971 after a certain amount of Ford 'productionisation'. US sales were slower than anticipated, with 1550 in 1972 and 2030 in 1973; and then came the energy crisis. This coupled with even stricter emission laws coming for 1975, forced Ford to stop importing the Pantera and close the Vignale plant in late 1974, by which time they had taken over de Tomaso's minority shareholding and had become owners of Ghia and Vignale. De Tomaso continued to build the Pantera in Modena

Latest de Tomaso is the Guara which employs a composite chassis with a mid-mounted 4-litre BMW V-8, which should give it a 160 mph maximum. Guara comes in coupé or roadster forms.

and has continued to update it ever since with more power, wider wheels and aerodynamic appendages.

Where the original 300 bhp Pantera would reach nearly 150 mph on the right gearing, the 1985 GT5-S clocked 160 mph. In 1990, the bodywork was restyled by Gandini and the engine had changed to the Ford 302 cu.in V-8 using fuel injection to give 305 bhp. You can still buy one in this form, or as the Pantera 200 with twin turbos and 530 bhp; the 200 denotes 200 mph, but no one has yet put this to the test.

Meanwhile de Tomaso launched the Guara in 1993, now available in open, coupé or Targa forms. Once again, it has a backbone chassis but this time in aluminium honeycomb and composites; 304 bhp comes from a 4.0-litre BMW V-8, which should give it a maximum speed around 160 mph.

SPECIFICATION	DE TOMASO PANTERA GT5-S
ENGINE	Ford V-8, 5752 cc
HORSEPOWER	350 bhp @ 6000 rpm
TRANSMISSION	Manual 5-speed
CHASSIS	Steel with glass-fibre bodywork
BRAKES	Discs all round
TOP SPEED	160 mph
ACCELERATION	**0-60 mph** 5.4 seconds **0-100 mph** 13.1 seconds

Throughout its long career, the Pantera displayed the virtues of Italian flair with old-fashioned, but economical, American muscle. It was fast, stylish, easy to maintain and established the de Tomaso name in the sports-car world. With the company now being run by the founder's son, Santiago, the Guara should keep the flag flying.

New style gave the old car a new lease of life with smoothed flanks and F40-style rear wing. It will continue to be available to special order.

FERRARI 365GTB4 DAYTONA

1971
174 mph
280 km/h

For ever known as the Daytona, the 365GTB4 was Ferrari's final fling for the front-engined two-seater; four-seaters would continue with front-mounted engines, but two-seater sports Ferraris would be mid-engined after this. But what a finale. It was a bold statement of sheer power and shameless aggression, from the sharp front end to the wide fastback that had lost any semblance of its predecessor's narrow cabin, inset from a curvaceous waist-line. It was a big car too, heavy and bulky, but a muscle car designed to appeal to the American market; its performance and maximum speed would leave all of those and the Europeans standing – it was king of the road in its day.

Its predecessor had been the 275GTB4. The 250GT series, running from 1954-64, had marked the transition from race-cars adapted for the road to purpose-built road cars; the 275s were the first Ferraris to be designed and developed from the outset as road cars. As ever, the type number referred to the capacity of a single cylinder; last of the original small-block engines, the 275 was a V-12 3.3-litre mounted in the front. Unlike previous road cars, it had the gearbox, now with five speeds, mounted in the rear – a transaxle – to keep the weight distribution more even. The chassis followed the familiar tubular frame principles but finally moved with the times and had independent rear suspension.

Announced at the 1964 Paris Show it was available in two body forms, the open 275GTS and the coupé 275GTB with 250-275 bhp. It was at the 1966 Paris Show that the final version was launched, the 275GTB4 for four overhead camshafts, two per bank of six cylinders; with 300 bhp at 8000 rpm it would run to 160 mph. It was a fast and agile car with an almost comfortable ride.

But while the 4-cam was launched in October 1966, extending the life of the 275, the new 330 range had been presented in March of that year. With the traditional V-12 single-cam stretched with a new longer block, the 300 bhp 4-litre was used to power the 330GTC and GTS. The chassis remained similar to that of the 275, but the drive-line incorporated a torque tube. The new body style featured a lower waistline with deeper windows, a notchback tail treatment and an oval

SPECIFICATION	FERRARI 365GTB4 DAYTONA
ENGINE	Aluminium V-12, 4390 cc
HORSEPOWER	352 bhp @ 7500 rpm
TRANSMISSION	Manual 5-speed
CHASSIS	Steel frame
BRAKES	Discs all round
TOP SPEED	174 mph
ACCELERATION	**0-60 mph** 5.4 seconds **0-100 mph** 12.6 seconds

Last of Ferrari's front-engined two-seater coupés, the Daytona was a magnificent charger in the right hands.

grille more reminiscent of the superamerica series. The same engine had been used in the mid-engined sports-racing 330P in 1964; the factory continued to develop the 4-litre engine but produced a 4.4-litre 365P for the non-works teams for 1965. The ultimate factory development came with the 1967 330P4 which had twin cams per bank with each cylinder having three valves and twin plugs plus fuel injection to generate 450 bhp at 8200 rpm; privateers made do with 380 bhp at

7300 rpm with carburetters and single-cam 365s. Ferrari won the world championship three times in those four years, including victory at Daytona for the 330P and 330P4.

First production car to use the 4.4-litre single-cam V-12 was the 365GT 2+2, an extremely elegant Pininfarina stretch of the 330GTC with an extra 25 cm in the wheelbase but 58 cm more in overall length to provide more luggage space as well as the extra seats; it also had self-levelling rear suspension. The 330GTC and GTS had to wait until late 1968 to be uprated to 365-series.

However, the big event of that year was the arrival of the ultimate two-seater coupé; Ferrari had profited from the racing experience in selecting its engine specification – the 4.4-litre with twin-cams per bank but only two valves, six carburetters and dry sump lubrication to produce a remarkable 352 bhp, 30 more than the single-cam cars. The chassis was basically that of the 330/365GTC. And the style set it off to perfection; early cars had the headlights visible behind a band of clear plastic running across the nose, but later cars had this replaced by body-colour metal and the headlamps became pop-ups. Other variants included a convertible – 100 only – and the 365GTC4, a 2+2 Daytona with less horsepower and a revised front end which was available in 1971/2 following the phasing out of the previous 2+2. But the Daytona stayed in production until 1974; over 1300 were built in that six-year period.

Just over 100 Spiders were made by the factory, but some Daytonas have since been decapitated to capture the same open elegance.

'It was a bold statement of sheer power and shameless aggression.'

FERRARI 288GTO

1986

189 mph

304 km/h

Smaller and a little more powerful than the flagship Testarossa, the 288GTO was the fastest Ferrari in its day. It should have been – it was designed as a racer. GTO? Gran Turismo Omologato or, in somewhat less evocative terms, Homologated GT. Homologation is the process of certifying that a number of identical units have been made; road cars are homologated by transport ministries when they conform to regulations; road-based race cars are homologated for competition by the FIA, the ruling body of motor sport, once a specified number have been built.

Over 1959-61, Ferrari had been building the short-wheelbase 250GT for road and competition use; when the FIA announced a GT championship for 1962, Ferrari needed something lower and lighter. The rules of the day stated that 100 identical cars should be built in 12 consecutive months, but that special bodied versions could be made once the 100 had been completed; the 250GT had already been accepted as a GT car, so the new car was submitted for approval with the revised bodywork. When the form came back stamped GT – Omologato, the name stuck. The 3-

variation in axle ratio and states of tune; factory cars may have achieved over 170 mph at Le Mans, but 165 mph is about right for 280 bhp.

Twenty years on and the FIA again introduced rules to encourage road-going GT cars to take part in racing and rallying with effect from 1982. This time the minimum quantity was 200 in a year for Group B. Ferrari had racing in mind, Porsche planned to race and rally the 959 while the rest of the competitive manufacturers built outrageous four-wheel-drive rally specials. In the event, Group B racing failed to capture any following and Group B rallying stopped in 1986 when the cars became too fast for their own – and spectator – safety. However Ferrari introduced the 288GTO at the 1984 Geneva Show as a Limited Edition of 200 and started taking deposits there and then.

While there was no homologation-inspired need to develop a previous design, Ferrari started with the 308GTB as the basis. Turbocharging small engines had become the fashion for ultimate power to weight ratios and Ferrari already made a 208 Turbo for the Italian market to avoid the heavy luxury tax on cars over 2-litres; so the

The latter-day GTO's rear wing vents are the only styling cue carried forward from the original 250GTO.

litre V-12 250GTO with 280+ bhp went on to win the new championship in 1962-4; while around 160 250GTs were built there were only 35 250GTOs. As most of these were road registered at some time in their lives, it is fair to record their figures as production cars but hard to establish representative ones as there is considerable

engine chosen was the V-8, set at 2.85-litres such that, like Porsche, the car would fit into the 4-litre category once the FIA's turbo correction factor of 1.4 was applied. With twin IHI turbochargers it would develop 400 bhp at 7000 rpm, but much more for racing, simply by adjusting turbo pressures. To allow a conventional racing gearbox behind the axle line, the engine was sited fore and aft which necessitated an extra 4 inches in the wheelbase. What had been the 308GTB's 225/50 x 16 rear tyres were used on the front of the GTO, with 265/50 x 16 tyres on the rear – so the body was flared out to accommodate them and any later increase, to the tune of an extra 7 inches. The chassis was just a stretched version of the 308's tubular frame, but the body was a mixture of materials using glass-fibre, Kevlar for the bonnet, and carbon/Kevlar for the roof. The car's weight

All mod cons are shown inside this genuine road car.

was quoted at 1160 Kg; although production ones with full interior trim were nearer 1300 Kg they were still 50 kg lighter than the 308GTB.

In looks the GTO was very similar to the 308, just longer and wider, until you came to the rear; the two or three near vertical slots, cut into the 250GTO's flanks behind the front wheels, became three similar cut-outs behind the 288GTO's rear wheels, and the tail spoiler, too, carried overtones of 20 years earlier. While the earlier car was designed for competition and won, the 288GTO was designed for competition but never ran – that hasn't stopped it from being another instant classic Ferrari.

'The 288GTO was the fastest Ferrari in its day.'

SPECIFICATION	FERRARI 288GTO
ENGINE	Aluminium V-8, twin turbos, 2855 cc
HORSEPOWER	400 bhp @ 7000 rpm
TRANSMISSION	Manual 5-speed
CHASSIS	Steel frame, composite body
BRAKES	Discs all round
TOP SPEED	189 mph
ACCELERATION	**0-60 mph** 5.0 seconds **0-100 mph** 11.0 seconds

Recognisably a longer, wider 308GTB, the 288GTO uses some carbon fibre panels in unstressed areas; the turbocharged 2.85-litre V-8 sits fore-and-aft.

FERRARI F512M

1995
191 mph
307 km/h

'The design has tried to move with the times, but the times have now overtaken the design.'

Below and below right: F512M has a revised front end with exposed lamps and a 'happier' intake; it is also a little faster than the otherwise similar TR.

Maybe the 512 is neither the most practical nor the nimblest of Ferraris, but it still has an almighty presence that shouts Ferrari; 78 inches wide, 44 inches low it still manages to be graceful in its Pininfarina clothes; and with 440 bhp from its flat-12 (boxer) 5-litre midships engine, it is also very fast but user-friendly with it. If Ferrari didn't keep producing even more exciting, but considerably less practical, devices like the 288GTO and the F40/50, the 'Berlinetta Boxer' would have attracted the stronger following which its all-round ability deserves; those that can afford them don't usually buy a big Ferrari for its practicality, and the others offer more short-term exhilaration.

The Boxer genre started life back in 1973 when the Daytona was still in production. Ferrari was never one to leap into new technologies, although the company has always been good at perfecting them once proven – a sound small-company philosophy. Thus Ferrari was beaten to the mid-engined road car draw by Lamborghini; such was caution that both the mid-engined Ferraris were to be shown as styling exercises well ahead of possible production as a means of sampling public opinion before taking the plunge.

Its first public airing was at the 1971 Turin Show, two years before the production launch.

At the time the *Grand Prix* and Sports-prototype racing cars were using a 3-litre flat-12 which gave a usefully low centre of gravity. It was a good configuration for a road car, too, giving a low rear deck height for better visibility but it dictated quite a wide car; however Ferrari preferred to keep the masses between the wheelbase and lifted the engine to put the gearbox within the rear of the sump – practicality ruled over the last word in handling and the model has lived with that ever since. While the engine followed the layout of the 3-litre, its dimensions and many of its components came from the 365 V-12 Daytona unit, although its camshafts were belt driven; with 344 bhp, it was slightly less powerful than the Daytona with a lower compression ratio but would pull similar speeds – *Motor* recorded 172 mph. Its style was unique, neither a big Dino nor a preview of the 308, with matt black below a line from the sharp nose to the rear bumper, set under the short stubby tail. Its title was a mouthful – 365GT4BB, Berlinetta Boxer denoting the different layout from that of the 365GTB4 Daytona. That first model was usually known as the Boxer, even though all subsequent models used a boxer engine.

The first update came in 1976; in response to restrictive emission legislation the capacity was increased to 5-litres for no power increase, the engine was fitted with a dry sump, and the rear tyre size was increased – these had been the same size front and rear on the first car – adding also to body width; a front spoiler helped to keep the nose down at high speeds. This became the 512, following the new numbering system of capacity followed by number of cylinders; the fuel injection 512i followed in 1981, again with no power increase. The first major change came in 1984 with a dramatically revised shape whose major feature was the side-strakes leading to intakes for the radiators which had been moved from the front to

just ahead of the rear wheels; the front intake stayed as a feed for brake cooling ducts. The 5-litre engine adopted 4 valves per cylinder to recover emission strangled outputs and generated 390 bhp; its heads were painted red to justify the revived Testarossa name. These changes, plus bigger rear tyres, widened the car by six inches, put another two inches in the wheelbase and increased the overall length by five inches – it had become a big car. It was faster, too, with a maximum around 182 mph.

Since then it has had minor styling changes with small power increases. For 1992 the 512TR had 428 bhp and anti-lock brakes, and the front showed a family identity that would be carried across to the 355. Only two years later came the F512M, recalling the 'Modificata' version of the 1970 racing GT car, with 440 bhp in slightly less weight, new wheels and a revised front with headlights now visible behind clear plastic; on the road, it should be fractionally faster than the earlier car, an estimated 191 mph against 188 mph. The overall shape, though, is unchanged from the 512TR. The design has tried to move with the times, but the times have now overtaken the design; the F355 is more agile and almost as fast and Ferrari are replacing the Big Boxer with a modern Daytona, a two-seater version of the front-engined 456GT labelled F555.

SPECIFICATION	FERRARI F512M
ENGINE	Aluminium flat-12, 4942 cc
HORSEPOWER	440 bhp @ 6750 rpm
TRANSMISSION	Manual 5-speed
CHASSIS	Steel frame, aluminium body
BRAKES	Discs all round
TOP SPEED	191 mph (307 km/h)
ACCELERATION	**0-60 mph** 4.8 seconds **0-100 mph** 10.2 seconds

When the Testarossa replaced the 512BB, those memorable side-strakes changed the styling from the bland to the exotic; the 512TR (above) and M have kept them.

FERRARI F50

1995
202 mph
325 km/h

'It is a real racer for the road, not a grand tourer.'

The Ferrari F50 is an out-and-out racer for the road, not a developed road car. The new V-12 engine is bolted direct to the carbon-fibre composite chassis. Despite more power than the F40, maximum speed will be no greater – ground effect is more important.

To the world of motoring, Ferrari means fast. Having someone else build the fastest road car doesn't go down too well in the corridors of power at Maranello, even if the racing heritage of the prancing horse transcends all other contenders. While the Ferrari 288GTO had topped the fastest Countach, the mid-'eighties saw the Porsche 959 at the head of the field. Ferrari responded with the F40 in 1988 with all but 200 mph. All were to be engulfed by the rash of supercars that flooded a diminishing market – Jaguar, Bugatti and McLaren cleared 200 mph comfortably. Ferrari has returned to the fray with the F50, but not to challenge the rest for maximum speed; the new car is an unashamed *Grand Prix* car for the road. They plan to build just 349 in three years; there were only 270 GTOs but over 1300 F40s.

The dramatic success of the limited edition 288GTO had suggested that the market would still absorb a large number of even faster cars bearing the prancing horse. With the GTO Evolution still-born by the lack of anywhere to race Group B cars, Ferrari had a sound base for the car that would celebrate 40 years of production. The chassis followed the tubular space-frame principles of the GTO but bonded carbon-fibre replaced the welded sheet steel boxing to give a lighter, stronger structure; body panelling and interior trims also benefited from modern composites. While the suspension was similar to that of the GTO, it was modified for Pirelli's latest P Zeros which were considerably wider; so track and car-width increased too. Power was also greater; using the same basic 308 unit but with larger bore, shorter stroke and higher turbo pressures, the output rose to 478 bhp at 7000 rpm from the 2936 cc V-8.

With all the weight reduction and near 20% power increase, it was not surprising that the F40 was very much quicker off the mark with 0-100 mph in 7.6 seconds against the GTO's 11.0 seconds; the top speed too rose from 189 to around 200 mph. On the road the F40 was tremendously fast and responsive with levels of roadholding that could only be explored on the track.

But take the new F50 to the Ferrari test track at Fiorano and it is 4 seconds a lap faster. That is what the new car is all about – a little faster in acceleration with similar top speed, but with *Grand Prix* technology to give real race-car roadholding.

The chassis is a carbon-fibre monocoque to which the engine is solidly bolted, acting as a stressed member to carry the rear suspension loads

through the final drive casing, which doubles as an oil tank, between engine and the new six-speed gearbox. Like a GP car, the springs are laid across the top of the casing and operated by push-rods. The front suspension also uses push-rod operated transverse springs and is mounted directly onto the monocoque via aluminium inserts. Both front and rear damping is electronically controlled according to speed and dynamic forces. While the V-12 engine uses the same 65 degree angle between the banks as the 456, it is based more on the normally-aspirated 1993 *Grand Prix* engine with 5 valves per cylinder operated by chain-driven camshafts. Developing 513 bhp from 4.7-litres, its output per litre is even higher than that of the F355.

Carbon-fibre, Kevlar and honeycomb are used for the bodywork, which is wind-tunnel developed to provide a downforce balancing that from the underbody venturis; the full width rear wing and the high-lighted panel-joint line are features that link the F50 to the F40. Inside, there is naked carbon-fibre with just a little soft trim while LCD instrumentation panel gives bar graphs for minor displays but needles for rev counter and a speedometer which reads to 360 km/h! The car comes in two forms, closed with an integrated roll-bar, or open with roll-hoops emerging from the twin head-fairings. It is a real racer for the road, not a grand tourer.

The F50 comes in two forms; the coupé and the sports-racing spider. The picture above shows the cabin of the spider.

Below: Based on the Evolution (competition) version of the GT0, the F40 was produced in greater numbers than its predecessor.

SPECIFICATION	FERRARI F40	FERRARI F50
ENGINE	Twin turbo V-8, 2936 cc	V-12, 4698 cc
HORSEPOWER	478 bhp @ 7000 rpm	513 bhp @ 8000 rpm
TRANSMISSION	Manual 5-speed	Manual 6 speed
CHASSIS	Steel and composites	Carbon-fibre
BRAKES	Discs all round	Discs all round
TOP SPEED	198 mph (319 km/h)	202 mph (325 km/h)
ACCELERATION	**0-60 mph** 4.1 seconds **0-100 mph** 7.6 seconds	3.9 seconds 7.2 seconds

FERRARI F355

1994

178 mph

286 km/h

'The F355 became an altogether different car from its predecessors.'

It often happens. Small cars get bigger with each model change until finally the former top of the range gets pushed out of the list. We still have the Ferrari F512M, but the latest F355 is very little slower than the bigger car, quicker in the 0-60 mph dash and a lot more agile on the road. It is a supercar in its own right, not just a little relation lurking in the shadows.

That was certainly how its ancestor started; the little Dino 246 wasn't even called a Ferrari, although it was named after Enzo's son. Its concept was first shown as a Pininfarina styling exercise on a mid-engined 2-litre racing chassis in 1965; three years later it finally went into production as the 206GT using an aluminium twin ohc 2-litre V-6 designed by Ferrari, but built by Fiat, as 500 were required for it to be used as a Formula 2 engine. Fiat were to install it in the two front-engined Fiat Dinos, a Pininfarina open two seater and a Bertone 2+2, but Ferrari decided to use it as well for the

Seeking a necessarily heavier four-seater version for 1973, Ferrari chose an aluminium 3-litre V-8, dimensionally two-thirds of a 365 V-12, but with its twin overhead cams driven by toothed belts; this was installed in the first Bertone-designed production Ferrari, the 308 GT4 with 8 inches extra in the wheelbase. Unlike the unitary 246GT chassis, the 308GT4 had a steel frame with glass-fibre bodywork; although never as acclaimed as the two-seaters, the GT4 stayed in production until 1980. Meanwhile, as Porsche continued to increase their engine sizes, the two-seater 246GT, which had been joined by the Targa-top GTS in 1972, was replaced by the 308GTB and GTS in 1975 using the same 255 bhp V-8 which propelled all models into the 150+ mph category – early models used glass-fibre bodywork but switched back to steel in 1977. Pininfarina's 308GTB took some cues from the big mid-engined 365GTBB and has long been rated as one of his best ever styles.

Fuel injection replaced carburetters in 1980 in the search for lower emission levels; the resultant power loss was to some extent mitigated by the 1982 adoption of 4-valve heads, although power was still 15 bhp down on the original. Meanwhile the GT4 had been replaced by the

This 1995 F355GTS features a removable roof panel.

new entry-level Ferrari for the Porsche market – the first mid-engined road Ferrari. For this, the engine was set transversely with the gearbox contained in the rear of the sump. When the required numbers had been completed – they won two F2 races in 1968 – Fiat increased the capacity to 2.4-litres using a cast-iron block which was adopted for both the Fiat and Ferrari Dinos. Ferrari's Dino 246 was a great success – an agile little jewel capable of around 145 mph.

more spacious, Pininfarina designed, Mondial in 1980 with a cabriolet coming in 1984. Power was more than restored with the 1985 change to 3.2-litres for the 328 range with changes to body and interior within a similar overall shape. In 1989 the capacity was further enlarged to 3.4-litres with new castings and the engine was mounted fore-and-aft, which also allowed it to sit lower so the 348 tb and ts thus had a 10 cm longer wheelbase; the new body style used Testa Rossa side strakes and a more pronounced intake grille shape. With the 3.4-litre engine initially producing 300 bhp, increased to 320 in 1993 shortly after the open-top Spider 348 was introduced, the new range could comfortably clear 160 mph – the Dino name had been dropped mid-way through the 308 series.

Good though the 348 was, the Honda NSX and Porsches had also benefited from considerable development, so Ferrari moved on several stages with the next car, the F355 which came in mid-1994. Taking the engine out to 3.5-litres and adding 5-valve heads pushed the power up to 380 bhp at 8250 rpm, 1000 rpm higher than the 348 needed for its 320 bhp, and then, the highest output per litre of any non-turbo engine; it thus needed a six-speed gearbox to make the best use of the higher rev range. The chassis, too, had changes with electronic damping control and a *Grand Prix*

style underbody venturi. The F355 became an altogether different car from its predecessors, a supercar in any model range except Ferrari.

SPECIFICATION	FERRARI F355
ENGINE	Aluminium V-8, 3496 cc
HORSEPOWER	380 bhp @ 8250 rpm
TRANSMISSION	Manual 6-speed
CHASSIS	Unitary steel
BRAKES	Discs all round with ABS
TOP SPEED	178 mph (286 km/h)
ACCELERATION	**0-60 mph** 4.6 seconds **0-100 mph** 10.6 seconds

Above: Open F355 adds pose appeal to this remarkable small Ferrari.

Diverging from recent Ferrari numerology, what should have been the 358 became the F355 as 3.5-litre 5-valve. With 380 bhp the little Ferrari is almost as fast as the flat-12 512TR.

FERRARI 456GT

1994

187 mph

301 km/h

'Inside is all the luxury you expect from the target class.'

Fast-back shape recaptures the Daytona, but the 456GT is a thoroughly modern Grand Tourer capable of covering long distances in quiet comfort.

Four-seater Ferraris are a rarity. The name is so bound up with racing and ultimate road-cars that a family Ferrari is almost a contradiction in terms. But, with the latest 456GT, the company has managed to create a genuine four-seater that behaves like a sports car – it was the last project in which Enzo Ferrari had direct involvement before his death in 1988. It is much more a direct descendant of the Daytona – or the matching 365GTC4 – than a development of the 400 series which came to a halt in 1989; there was a three year gap before the 456GT was launched.

Emphasising the commitment to provide a genuine on-going front-engined range, a new engine was developed; once more a V-12 with 456 cc per cylinder – using the old-style numbering for the model name – this has a 65 degree angle between the banks which carry four-valve heads with toothed belt cam drive; a dry sump system has been retained to keep the engine low. A new 6-speed transaxle was designed too. Pininfarina's new shape follows the fastback contours of the Daytona rather than the square-rigged 400 and it must have a very low drag-factor as the 442 bhp unit propels the car to over 300 km/h, only a little slower than the factory claim for the mid-engined 512M. In keeping with the fast tourer aspect, the suspension is electronically adjustable for ride

firmness, and road noise has been well subdued. Inside is all the luxury you expect from the target class, traditional light leather but no wooden fillets; to assist getting into the rear seats, you tilt the front seats and they move forward automatically on their runners. And there is a deep luggage boot which comes with its own fitted luggage. It's a really *grand* tourer.

Not that the previous series were wrong in their time, but they were more like stretched sports coupés than purpose-built comfortable fast tourers. Between the 400s and the long sleek 365GT 2+2 came the 365GT4 2+2; the 4 denoted the adoption of the twin-cam heads, albeit for fashion rather than performance. But the body was an all-new more modern clean-cut shape without the sinuous curves of its predecessor; slightly shorter in overall length, it nevertheless had a longer wheelbase to provide a little more rear seat room. That stayed in production from 1972-75 before the 400 arrived as a 4.8-litre – a longer stroke – in a revised version of the previous body; what made it more remarkable, though, was that it was the first Ferrari to be offered with automatic transmission and most were equipped with the General Motors unit. The previous model hadn't been certified for the American market, but this was designed for it.

Fuel injection was added to make the 400i in 1979 in the interests of refinement and emission control and at the expense of a power drop from 340 to 315 bhp, but the basic 400 had a ten year run through to 1985. The 4.9-litre 412 followed on with further body and interior refinements for a further four years; by then it had become a genuinely comfortable fast tourer for those who had grown out of the two-seaters, but, after 17 years of the same basic design and shape, it wasn't going to bring in fresh Ferrari owners – a fresh approach was needed to put a four-seater Ferrari into a market that had such effective cars as the Mercedes 600SL and BMW 850 at its bottom end or the Bentley Continental R at the top. In 1987 it was a difficult time to make such a decision, as the supercar market was at its height and Ferrari didn't want to be lured into producing significantly

more than 3000 cars a year should demand continue; in the event, the investment-led market crashed and Ferrari made the right decision to continue with a broad range. The reception given to the 456GT has proved the point; all it needs now is automatic transmission for the US market and this would be likely to take the form of an electronic clutch with matching engine management like the 1993 *Grand Prix* cars. Racing always improves Ferrari's breed.

Little changed in style from the 1975 400, this 412 was the forerunner of the 456 with similar rear seat space.

Light Italian leather is tastefully used throughout the car. Rear seats have enough headroom for adults so the 456GT is better than most of its rivals.

SPECIFICATION	FERRARI 456GT
ENGINE	Aluminium V-12, 5474 cc
HORSEPOWER	442 bhp @ 6250 rpm
TRANSMISSION	Manual 6-speed
CHASSIS	Steel frame, aluminium body
BRAKES	Discs all round with ABS
TOP SPEED	187 mph
ACCELERATION	**0-60 mph** 5.1 seconds **0-100 mph** 11.6 seconds

FERRARI 550 MARANELLO

1996
199 mph
320 km/h

An exercise of refined traditionalism, the front-engine/rear-drive V-12 engined 550 Maranello benefits from state-of-the-art mechanicals as well as electronics. The aluminium bodywork is, as ever, by Pininfarina but there is only room for two seats. Beneath is a tubular steel frame.

Practicality is the keynote of the 550 Maranello coupé of 1996, that is Ferrari's first front-engined two-seater for close on 30 years. But there's nothing conservative about the model's top speed which is claimed to be 199 mph.

This car is very much the brainchild of Ferrari's president, Luca di Montezemolo, and to place the 550 in context it is necessary to retrace our steps to the time of his 1992 appointment.

Then the company's range included two mid-engined two-seaters; the flat-12-powered 512 TR and its cheaper 348 stablemate which employed a V-8 unit. Both cars were very similar in concept with the only differences being price and performance.

Such a race-bred engine location offers its driver a better handling car than a front-engined one but this is at the expense of loss of interior accommodation and luggage capacity with an attendant rise in noise levels.

The 550 was intended to address these limitations to provide a more conventional and usable product than the 512M it replaced. The result is a superlative grand tourer rather than an uncompromising sports car.

Ferrari has been wedded to the V-12 engine since its 1947 inception. The 5.5-litre aluminium unit – the capacity is reflected in the model's name – with its twin overhead-camshafts per bank and attendant four valves per cylinder, is shared with its four-seater 465GT stablemate that is also front-engined.

However, the internal mechanicals are peculiar to the new model, most significantly the lighter pistons and titanium connecting rods to permit higher revolutions.

A further refinement is provided by the presence of hydraulic tappets, an innovation for Ferrari, that are both quieter and more efficient from an emissions standpoint.

There is also a variable-intake manifold, that is peculiar to the 550, which gives the model its own very distinctive characteristics, when compared with the 456. The purpose-designed intake system incorporates no less than 12 throttle valves actuated by electro-pneumatic servos controlled by a Bosch computerised brain.

Since 1964 Ferraris have featured a rear-mounted gearbox and the 550 similarly has a transaxle that incorporates a 456-derived six-speed unit.

The two-door aluminium body is, inevitably, by Pininfarina with retro elements, not perhaps the most memorable of designs to spring from this respected styling house but one with a sculpted bonnet and strong wing line to emphasise the

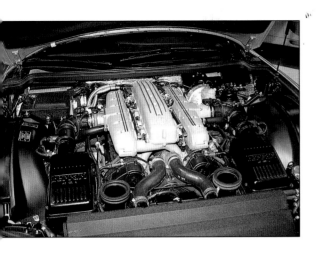

hidden mechanicals. The use of composites is confined to the bumpers and wheel arches liners. Drag coefficient is a creditable 0.33.

This finely-honed shape conceals a chassis of chrome-moly tubular steel which is similar to that used on the 456. Suspension is by the customary all-round, unequal length wishbones with massive Brembo drilled disc brakes.

These have benefited from Formula 1 technology which means that the 550's progress is arrested by four-pot aluminium calipers with special heat insulating pistons that prevents the fluid from boiling, even after extreme applications.

There is an electrically-controlled traction system and the driver has a choice of two settings: Normal and a firmer Sport. This, along with the front-engine/rear-drive configuration, makes a significant contribution to the 550's handling, which is outstanding.

No Ferrari would be complete without being fitted with handsome magnesium wheels and the 550's five-spoked ones are shod with big, beefy 18-inch tyres.

The Ferrari owner and passenger can get in and out of this two-seater with ease, which is significant because some of the visually stunning,

but lower slung, mid-engined models have represented something of a challenge in this respect!

Interior trim is restrained but luxurious with finely upholstered natural-hued leather seats and matching carpeting, black-faced instruments and fascia. Steering is, of course, power assisted and a little over two turns from lock to lock.

The gear lever operates in Ferrari's traditional exposed gate although, for the 1998 season, the model will be available with the company's Formula 1-related Selespeed gearbox.

The clutch pedal will accordingly disappear and gear changes will be effected by the driver operating two paddles positioned behind, and either side of, the rim of the steering wheel – just like on Ferrari's racing cars.

There are no rear seats, but luggage (secured by a pair of leather straps) can be carried on a carpeted shelf that sits above the 114-litre petrol tank which also takes up most of the boot space. This is necessary because the 550 gulps down fuel at an average rate of 7.9 mpg when being used around town although this figure improves to an overall 13 when motorway journeys are taken into account.

Turning the scales at 1960 kg, according to Ferrari the 550 can reach 60 mph in a formidable 4.3 seconds which is half a second less than the 512. Its official blistering 199 mph top speed is an eight miles per hour improvement on that of its mid-engined predecessor.

Priced on its announcement at £143,685, the 550 is over £50,000 more than the V-8-powered 355 but the top line Formula 1-related F50 is well over twice the price . . .

The Maranello also marks the arrival of names for Ferrari models, which in the past had often simply featured a number. The choice is most appropriate in this case because Maranello is the model's birthplace and the name of the small town in northern Italy where the factory is located. But Ferraris are for the fortunate few: just 3000 or so cars leave the works every year.

Left: The 5.5-litre, dry sump, V-12 engine has twin overhead camshafts per cylinder bank and, accordingly, four valves per cylinder. Based on the 456 model, further refinement is provided by hydraulic tappets. A Bosch M 5.2 electronic management system is employed.

Purposeful and restrained, the 550's interior is upholstered in the finest leather. The front engine location ensures this is a spacious two-seater. Note the traditional Ferrari gearchange gate. A rear-mounted, six-speed 'box is used with an automatic version in the offing.

'According to Ferrari the 550 can reach 60 mph in a formidable 4.3 seconds.'

SPECIFICATION	FERRARI 550 MARANELLO
ENGINE	Aluminium V-12, 5474 cc
HORSEPOWER	479 bhp @ 7000 rpm
TRANSMISSION	Manual 6-speed
CHASSIS	High tensile moly-tubular
BRAKES	Discs all round with ABS
TOP SPEED	199 mph (320 km/h)
ACCELERATION	**0-60 mph** 4.6 seconds **0-100 mph** 10.1 seconds

FORD GT40 MK III

1966
164 mph
264 km/h

'A handful of Mk IIIs were made to provide proper street-legal motoring.'

Arguably the first of the mid-engined supercars, the Ford GT40 was designed as a racer but racing rules forced it to spawn a road-going derivative. Single-seater racing car design had changed over from the traditional front-engined layout in the late 'fifties, led by Cooper and confirmed by Lotus. The racing sports cars followed from 1960, but these were racers not road cars; putting an engine immediately behind the driver wasn't considered practical for a road car with poor visibility and nowhere to put the luggage, noisy too – with little space within the engine compartment for silencers. By the time they came to produce a real road version, Ford quietened the car considerably, made its lighting road-legal, and created a luggage box in the engine compartment – anything in there was going to get hot, a problem for the occupants too.

The Ford GT40 – 40-inches high – was a product of the merged interests of Ford of America and Lola Cars to produce an endurance race winner – Le Mans in particular. Eric Broadley's Lola GT ran with Ford power in the 1963 season at which time Ford had been working on their own GT car since mid-1962, having been thwarted in a bid to buy Ferrari. The GT40 arrived for the 1964 season; built at a new British subsidiary, Ford Advanced Vehicles, its glass-fibre body concealed a stiff sheet steel chassis carrying a 4.2-litre Ford V-8 mated to an Italian Colotti gearbox and all the suspension used race-style double wishbones. The first year wasn't a great success until Ford handed over the development and racing to Carroll Shelby's Shelby American while Ford continued work on the Mark II.

For 1965, the GT40 adopted the 4727 cc Ford V-8 tuned to around 380 bhp and used a German ZF gearbox. While the cars had some success, they failed at Le Mans as did the Mk IIs which had 485 bhp 7-litre engines. With a new

sports car category scheduled for 1966, FAV had begun to build the necessary 50 GT40s while work continued in America on the Mk II cars as contenders for outright victory; the big cars went on to win Le Mans and the championship in 1966. The Mk IV development won the French race again in 1967. Ford's first target was achieved within just three years of racing; after the second victory the company retired from this form of racing, leaving others to campaign the GT40 in sports car racing until 1969 when the rules changed again and the car became outdated. However the GT40 was to win Le Mans in 1968 and 1969 as a final fling.

Ford Advanced Vehicles had completed the necessary 50 in mid-1966 but went on to build

SPECIFICATION	FORD GT40 Mk III
ENGINE	Cast-iron V-8, 4727 cc
HORSEPOWER	306 bhp @ 6000 rpm
TRANSMISSION	Manual 5-speed ZF transaxle
CHASSIS	Steel frame, glass-fibre bodywork
BRAKES	Discs all round
TOP SPEED	164 mph
ACCELERATION	**0-60 mph** 5.3 seconds **0-100 mph** 11.8 seconds

A Slough-built roadgoing Mark III GT40 of 1966 identified by its reprofiled nose, modified headlights and front overriders. The mid-located, 4.7-litre V-8 was detuned to provide 306 bhp but was still able to reach 100 mph in under 12 seconds. Luggage was carried in a special container above the gearbox.

another 57. Some 30 were built as road cars, just quieter racers on narrower tyres, but a handful of Mk IIIs were made to provide proper street-legal motoring. These had 306 bhp engines and different bodywork – new nose with four headlights, and a longer tail to allow the luggage space. Inside, the trim was somewhat more luxurious with some carpet and a radio, but it has to be said that even a racing GT40 was more comfortable than any other racer – Ford appreciated that uncomfortable cars are tiring to drive in endurance races.

With just 7 Mk IIIs produced but many racing cars converted to road use, it is not easy to find the performance figures for genuine Holley-carburetted 306 bhp cars. Given the right gearing, the 380 bhp cars with four Weber carburettors were able to reach nearly 200 mph at Le Mans; with 300 bhp they could be expected to reach 175 mph. However the road cars were available with a choice of axle ratios and most were sold with gearing more suited to everyday motoring, which limited the possible top speed to around 164 mph but gave very good acceleration. These figures came from *Motor* who tested a short-tailed Holley-carburettor car in 1968, but they are fast enough and it was a very enjoyable road car.

GT40s won Le Mans on four successive occasions, from 1966 to 1969. The latter year marked the end of GT40 production and this roadgoing example dates from then. Many drivers caught a glimpse of this rear view!

HONDA NSX

1990

160 mph

256 km/h

'The NSX is a superbly engineered driver's car with very safe handling and enough performance for most.'

Honda only began to produce four-wheelers in 1964, starting with mini-cars. Since then they have gradually built up to the level of a large-scale manufacturer with a full range of models that have also been produced in factories in America and England, where their contribution to Rover has been invaluable. But they wanted a flag-ship above the Legend range. They had the required technology, so why not produce a Japanese answer to Ferrari and Porsche?

Supercars of the mid-'eighties were essentially European and mostly Italian; most came from companies that had strong track records. Honda's own track record was as good as any on two wheels, while four-wheeled prowess encompassed a pair of *Grands Prix* victories with their own cars in 1965 (Mexican GP) and 1967 (Italian GP), the 1966 domination of Formula Two with the Brabham team plus the more recent manufacture of successful *Grands Prix* engines from 1983. If that isn't enough heritage, the NSX is out to create its own track record in GT racing – three were entered for the 1994 Le Mans as a trial run, and all finished. They will be back.

The new car had to be a practical technology showcase, a sensible pointer to the future; aluminium was used wherever possible – chassis, body, suspension were all aluminium via an appropriate process whether pressing, forging or casting. It had to be mid-engined but the V-6 was mounted transversely with the gearbox on the end, thus saving cockpit intrusion and allowing a decent amount of luggage to be carried behind. The engine is an all-aluminium four-cam V-6 3-litre which uses Honda's V-TEC variable valve timing and the VVIS variable intake volume systems, both of which allow good low speed torque and high power, 270 bhp at 7100 rpm in this case. Given that Honda joined the GP world in the turbo era, they might have used that technology to generate even more power, but 280 bhp was enough for Japanese legislation and the light weight ensured that acceleration was up to market standard – 1340 Kg.

Traction control and ABS were a necessary part of a high-tech chassis design, with speed-sensitive electrically operated assistance for the power steering; this was initially only available when the car was fitted with automatic transmission but became a no-cost option for manual transmission cars in 1994. At the same time, the wheels grew an inch in diameter and half an inch in width to take lower profile tyres.

Clothing all this mechanical sophistication is a pleasing enough shape that borrows cues from no-one, not even from Honda itself as there is little marque identity in the rest of the range. It scores against many mid-engined cars by having a compact enough engine to allow a flat rear deck for good visibility. It scores too in luggage space, at

3-litre V-6 sits transversely and there is room for luggage behind it.

the expense of an extended tail which carries a rear wing integrated with the body sides; the resulting deep and slightly detached rear section upsets the overall balance. But the shape obviously works, as the car achieves 160 mph on its 270 bhp.

However the proof of any pudding is in the eating and the NSX is a superbly engineered driver's car with very safe handling and enough performance for most. It is also very quiet and comfortable and has shown every evidence of being thoroughly reliable as an everyday car; that is now to be expected from any car in the Porsche, Mercedes market. Further appeal was added with

the 1995 introduction of the T-Roof, a removable top panel to match the Porsches and Ferraris.

A T-roof version became available in 1995 to give a boost to sales.

SPECIFICATION	HONDA NSX
ENGINE	Aluminium V-6, 2977 cc
HORSEPOWER	270 bhp @ 7100 rpm
TRANSMISSION	Manual 5-speed
CHASSIS	Unitary aluminium
BRAKES	Discs all round with ABS
TOP SPEED	160 mph
ACCELERATION	**0-60 mph** 5.3 seconds **0-100 mph** 12.6 seconds

Japan's only mid-engined supercar makes extensive use of aluminium in its chassis and body.

ISO GRIFO GL365

1966

161 mph

259 km/h

'It had plenty of effortless performance and a remarkable top speed.'

Styled by Giugiaro while at Bertone, the Bizzarrini-designed Grifo was one of the best-looking cars of its day; with 365 bhp from a Chevrolet V-8 it also went very well.

Even now, over 30 years after its first appearance at the 1963 Turin Show, the Iso Grifo A3L is a strikingly beautiful car. Low, wide and undeniably sleek, it was one of Giugiaro's creations while he worked with Bertone. Powered by a 365 bhp version of Chevrolet's 327 cu.in (5360 cc) V-8, it had plenty of effortless performance and a remarkable top speed, 10-15 mph faster than Astons and Jaguar E-types could manage with their highly tuned six-cylinder engines. American power had become fashionable with a number of the smaller specialist manufacturers – Facel Vega, Bristol and Jensen used Chrysler units, AC used Ford as would de Tomaso, and Gordon Keeble also used a Chevrolet 327.

In fact the Gordon-Keeble had preceded the first Iso by two years; in its original Gordon GT form it was shown at Geneva in 1960 with a nice four-seater body which was Giugiaro's first work for Bertone. Financial problems delayed its production for four years by which time it used a glass-fibre body. Meanwhile Count Renzo Rivolta was seeking to take Milan-based Iso back into motor manufacture after the Isetta bubble-car period; aiming at the luxury GT market, he approached Bertone and the result was shown at the 1962 Geneva Show – the Iso-Rivolta followed Giugiaro's earlier design remarkably closely, apart from a revised front and higher boot section.

Not only that, but the boxed tubular chassis design was very similar, right down to the de Dion rear suspension. This was developed by Giotto Bizzarrini who had established his own prototype-building company in 1962; project director of the Ferrari 250GTO he was also designing Lamborghini's first V-12 engine, all three projects in 1962. So let's just say . . . drawing inspiration from John Gordon's earlier prototype, Bizzarrini, Rivolta and Bertone brought the high-style Iso Rivolta 4-seater into production for 1963; using the softer 327 engine with 300 bhp coupled to the Borg Warner 4-speed manual box it would do 0-100 mph in 19 seconds and reach 135 mph. It was a fine car.

For the 1963 Turin Show, Bizzarrini shortened the chassis by 20 cm for Giugiaro to create the Iso Grifo 2-seater in two forms, the road going Luxury A3L and the sleeker more aerodynamic Competition A3C, similar in form but without a single interchangeable panel – it was the homologation special derivative as the Ferrari 250GTO was to the GT and Aston Martin Project 214 cars were to the DB4GT. Subsequently

The large rear window gave excellent visibility to this Italian muscle car.

Bizzarrini was to reverse the process and make a road-going A3C as the Bizzarrini Strada 5300 in coupé and convertible forms. However, solo A3C models competed at Le Mans in 1964 (14th) and 1965 (9th) and the 1964 car clocked 172 mph down the straight using over 400 bhp from a competition 327 fitted with Weber carburetters.

These cars ran in the prototype category as the required number had not been made by then; the first production A3L Grifos were built in 1965.

Although the 300 bhp Rivolta engine was an option, the standard A3L used the 365 bhp version with solid valve lifters for more revs and power – it would become known as the GL365. Further refinement with power was created for 1969 when the Corvette's 7-litre 427 cu.in engine was inserted with just over 400 bhp, hence the new model's Grifo GL400 designation.

While Iso replaced the Rivolta with the two-door Lele (Bertone) and the four-door Fidia (Giugiaro on behalf of Ghia) in 1969, the Grifo continued until 1974 by which time Bertone had built 411 of those stunning bodies. In that year the Rivolta family sold out to American interests which shortly collapsed. The Grifo was the car that ensures the name will be remembered.

SPECIFICATION	ISO GRIFO GL365
ENGINE	Cast-iron V-8, 5360 cc
HORSEPOWER	365 bhp @ 6200 rpm
TRANSMISSION	Manual 4-speed
CHASSIS	Steel frame
BRAKES	Discs all round
TOP SPEED	161 mph
ACCELERATION	**0-60 mph** 7.4 seconds **0-100 mph** 16.6 seconds

Like the four-seater Iso Rivolta, the Grifo was designed around big Chevrolet power.

JAGUAR D-TYPE

'For maximum speed they let it run through to 6600 rpm to clock 162 mph.'

Jaguar's Le Mans winning race-car may not be everyone's idea of a production road car but it qualifies on two counts. First, 45 were built for private customers for general competition; they were mostly registered for use on the road at the time and some never raced. And secondly, the XKSS was sold as a road-equipped version of the standard D-type competition car with identical performance. More than the 16 XKSS would have been built had not Jaguar suffered from that notorious factory fire of 1957; as it was, 61 customer cars were built over the period 1955-7 and the works used a further 17.

Generally, race cars are improved during their careers but customer D-types were rarely subjected to modifications of which the factory didn't approve; the one tested by the American *Road & Track* magazine in 1956 was a normal 260 bhp 3.4-litre D with a slightly shorter final drive than standard countered by oversize tyres to match the Jaguar fitment of a 3.54:1 axle ratio. Owned by Continental Motors of California, XKD528 was being raced by Pearce Woods, who seemed quite happy to ignore the factory rev limit of 5800 rpm for the tests; using 6200 rpm they were able to reach 60 mph in 4.7 sec still in first gear, and go on to 100 mph in 12.1 sec. For maximum speed they let it run through to 6600 rpm to clock 162 mph. This confirmed the 164 mph run which Phil Walters had made at Daytona Beach the year before in XKD406, shortly before he and Mike Hawthorn won the Sebring 12-hour race – a Le Mans type 2.79:1 axle ratio was used for that which dropped the revs to 5500 rpm. *Road & Track's* later test of an XKSS showed 149 mph and 0-100 mph in 13.6 sec. The highest speed ever recorded for a D-type was 185.5 mph at Bonneville in 1960 with a 3.8-litre engine and a 2.53:1 axle.

Although pre-war SS cars had been used in competitions, the works only seriously started competing with the XK120, launched in 1948. The XK120C came in 1951 as a purpose-built sports-racer using the same 3.4-litre twin ohc six-cylinder engine in a very different chassis under a new body. Le Mans victory then was the main goal and the C-type obliged in 1951 and 1953, among other victories. The D-type came in 1954 as another all-new car around the famous XK engine; this used an aeroplane-style central monocoque to which were attached sub-frames. Front and rear suspension followed C-type principles but with better location for the live rear axle. What set the D-type apart from any other period racer was the beautiful stream-lined body designed by aerodynamicist Malcolm Sayer; it combined proven function with elegance of form giving the high speed necessary for the Le Mans straights without seeming to suffer from high speed lift.

All the customer cars would retain the first style which would become known as 'short-nose' after the front of the 1955 factory cars was extended 7.5 inches for

Racer's cockpit. D-types had central division to mount a metal passenger-side cover. This was removed for the road-going XKSS which had full-width screen.

even better aerodynamics; these also had the famous tail-fins fared into the standard headrest. Le Mans victories came in 1955, 1956 and 1957 with many more besides; Jaguar had stopped running their own team but continued to provide engines and assistance to the Ecurie Ecosse and Cunningham teams as well as to the cars that used Jaguar engines, notably Lister.

While the D-type engine was basically that of the original 3442 cc XK120, it featured dry sump lubrication, special camshafts, bigger valves and triple Weber carburetters to produce 250 bhp at 5750 rpm in its production form whereas the XK140 – introduced in 1954 – had 190 bhp. The limitation was in the size of inlet valves that could be fitted; accordingly the wide-angle head was introduced with the inlet at 40 degrees to the vertical rather than 35, but this was not fitted to

the production cars. Works engines produced up to 280 bhp on carburetters. When the 3.8-litre engine became available in 1957, many earlier Ds were converted.

Following the 1960 Le Mans appearance of a modernised D-type labelled E2A, the famous E-type was launched in 1961 carrying many of the lessons learnt in the D-type's racing years. The ultimate 3.8-litre XK engine was that prepared for the Lindner-Nocker coupé with 344 bhp at 6500 rpm using Lucas fuel injection, some 40 bhp more than a D-type had ever used, and 37 per cent more than the production cars.

D-types came in two styles. This is a works long-nose as used by the 1955-7 Le Mans winners, complete with tail-fin head faring for high speed stability.

The XKSS was modelled on the short-nose D-types. This is XKD527 which was sold through the same American dealership as XKD528 which clocked 162 mph.

SPECIFICATION	JAGUAR D-TYPE
ENGINE	Straight 6, 3442 cc
HORSEPOWER	250 bhp @ 5750 rpm
TRANSMISSION	Manual 4-speed
CHASSIS	Central monocoque
BRAKES	Discs all round
TOP SPEED	162 mph
ACCELERATION	**0-60 mph** 4.7 seconds **0-100 mph** 12.1 seconds

JAGUAR XJ220

*'The XJ220 is
an electrifying
road car.'*

Sensation of the 1988 Birmingham Motor Show, the XJ220 aimed to set new standards of road-going performance with a 500bhp V-12 Jaguar engine mounted amidships and mated to a complex 5-speed four-wheel-drive transmission; and it looked like a Jaguar, too, with more than a hint of the still-born XJ13 sports-racer from the mid-'sixties. Conceived over the winter of 1984/5 by Engineering Director Jim Randle it was designed for International Group B racing. At that time Porsche had announced the 959 but hadn't built any, Ferrari had started building the 288GTO and Jaguar had made a tentative return to racing via the American Group 44 team competing in the American IMSA version of Group C; they would enter Group C in 1985 with Tom Walkinshaw Racing (TWR). The XJ220 would embody all that was necessary for successful Group B competition and add all the necessary road refinements too.

The original prototype was built behind the scenes, away from normal Jaguar work, with a few dedicated employees and a lot of help from the suppliers around Coventry, most notably FF Developments who supplied the transmission and the secret assembly area. That it was to take three years was due to the fact that work on it had to be fitted around normal Jaguar development. Jaguar's then chairman, John Egan, hadn't even seen the car until a week before that 1988 show.

Announced as a prototype of which perhaps two hundred and twenty could be built, the car soon had a flock of people trying to place orders with £50,000 deposits. Jaguar couldn't possibly build it among the production lines, so the project was handed over to JaguarSport, the joint Jaguar-TWR operation set up for niche variants and motor racing. By now Group B was going nowhere, so the last word in

racing technology was less important; TWR simplified the design, removing the 4WD, but sadly dropped the Jaguar V-12 in favour of the turbocharged 3.5-litre V-6 which would become the chosen unit for Group C racing for 1989/90. Having started life as the power unit for the MG Metro 6RV rally car, it just wasn't a Jaguar engine to the true enthusiast, and its racing life was to be short-lived. Other conceptual changes included shortening the car and using a chassis of aluminium honeycomb rather than sheet aluminium, but it still looked broadly the same, had even more power at 550 bhp and was 275 Kg lighter than the original.

A little over a year after its first showing, the heavily revised car was launched at £290,000 with a production quantity of 200-350. Three months later, in February 1990 this was confirmed at 350 with delivery to start two years later. Meanwhile, TWR had been gently developing a road-going version of the XJR-9 which had won the 1988 Group C championship powered by Jaguar V-12; this XJR9-R was running during 1989 and was finally announced as the XJR-15 in November 1990. While it was almost road-legal, it was launched for a one-make racing series, accompanying selected *Grand Prix* meetings, and

JaguarSport developed the XJR-15 as a potentially road-legal version of the Le Mans winning XJR-9 V-12 for use in a limited race series.

The original XJ220 prototype (left) was longer and heavier due to V-12 engine and four-wheel-drive system; there was little style adjustment between the two.

only 20 or so were to be built. There is no doubt that some of the potential XJ220 owners would have preferred a road-going version of a real Jaguar racer than even the ultimate road-car, but they had committed to their XJ220 purchase knowing it was powered by the turbo V-6 and the XJR-15 was not technically a road car. In fact, the racing career of the XJR-15 was not particularly notable, while the XJ220 is now embarking on its own racing as the international racing rules have changed again and the car is suited to them; a Le Mans win would change attitudes.

Meanwhile the XJ220 is an electrifying road car. When originally announced, it was claimed to be able to exceed 200 mph, reach 60 mph in 3.6 seconds and 100 mph in 8 seconds. In its final form it has clocked nearly 220 mph, and returned 3.5 and 7.9 seconds for 0-60 mph and 0-100 mph. It doesn't have four-wheel-drive, although FF also built the new gearbox, but it doesn't need it; thanks to aerodynamic down-force. While no longer such a technical *tour de force*, the XJ220 has delivered its promise to be the fastest ever Jaguar.

SPECIFICATION	JAGUAR XJ220
ENGINE	Turbo V-6, 3498 cc
HORSEPOWER	549 bhp @ 7000 rpm
TRANSMISSION	Manual 5-speed
CHASSIS	Aluminium honeycomb, ali body
BRAKES	Discs all round
TOP SPEED	217 mph
ACCELERATION	**0-60 mph** 3.6 seconds **0-100 mph** 7.9 seconds

As finally developed XJ220 had a turbocharged V-6 engine and two-wheel drive but met its performance targets.

JAGUAR XK8

1996
158 mph
254 km/h

'It is the E-type that the market wants to remember and the style reflects this.'

Like its E-type spiritual forebear, the XK8 is produced in both open and closed forms. Although this is a right-hand drive example, the majority will be sold in America.

It has been a long wait but Jaguar have finally produced the spiritual successor to the much revered, legendary E-type. The new XK8 may not develop its own track record, but it exactly matches the enthusiast's perception of a thoroughly modern version of the 'sixties sporting icon.

When Jaguar launched the E-type in 1961, it was quite obviously the production version of the racing D-type; the engine was almost the same, the monocoque chassis used the same principle and it looked very similar. Racing had improved Jaguar's road-going breed and development had made it a little more comfortable with independent rear suspension.

Adding a V-12 version in 1971 did not detract from the E-type's race-derived appeal although the design was getting a little long in the tooth. Others were more comfortable and had better road-holding. But when the XJS arrived, it was far from the F-type that enthusiasts were awaiting; they wanted an evolution E-type, not a short wheelbase XJ12 with funny headlights and curious rear sail panels.

However the XJS became a niche model in its own right and lasted 21 years. It wasn't a sports car in the E-type mould but it was a very comfortable, and very quiet, fast tourer. Latterly, JaguarSport had marketed some engine conversions and body kits that considerably altered the car's character for those still yearning for the modern E-type, while the factory came up with the 6.0-litre XJR-S capable of nearly 160 mph. Such developments removed some of the urgency for an XJS replacement but this was becoming increasingly overdue; in fact, Jaguar had planned to replace it around 1988 with XJ41 once the XJ40 – the 1986 XJ6 – was in production.

A number of XJ41 prototypes had been built, but it was finally decided that the cost of getting that car into production would be too great to amortize over the numbers that could be sold. To try and keep the project alive, Jaguar then put the new XJ41 body design onto the existing XJS platform. Initially it seemed that new owners, Ford, had stopped this one, too, as the concept was turned into a new small Aston Martin.

But Ford obviously had second Jaguar

thoughts as sporting cars became fashionable again. If some of the production costs could be shared with Aston Martin, then the XJ41-cum-XJS could rise again as X100. However Aston Martin had been given the six-cylinder option, albeit supercharged, so Jaguar's version needed a new engine; exhaust emissions, fuel thirst and weight were against the V-12, so the choice fell on a new, modern V-8 designed specifically for Jaguar – not just another version of an American quad-cam. Initial work started on Project X100 in January 1992, the green light came in October and the new car was unveiled at the Geneva Show in March 1996.

Although the official launch was scheduled for NEC 1996, Geneva was chosen for a preview because that was where the E-type had made its first appearance 35 years earlier. Although the car owes much of its chassis engineering to the XJS, it is the E-type that the market wants to remember and the style reflects this. The name too. The long 'bonnet' with the rounded intake is very much like the E-type, and the profile is similar to that of the fixed head coupés; it is a modern integrated design with retro appeal.

The new V-8 engine is a 4-litre with 4-valves per cylinder; with variable inlet cam timing it produces some 285 bhp with very good low speed pulling power. This is enough to give it a maximum speed around 158 mph; with the five-speed automatic fitted to all, the acceleration from rest is good enough but not as good as the Aston which is helped by manual transmission. It is a little faster than the original E-type but a lot more comfortable and faster versions can be expected to follow.

Just a month after the Geneva coupé launch, Jaguar displayed the convertible at the New York Show, as important a market for the XK8 as it was for the XKE.

The XK8, styled by Jaguar's Geoff Lawson, replaced the long running XJS and is the first new model to appear under Ford's stewardship of the respected British company.

The all new AJ-V8 engine was designed by Jaguar and, as such, shares no components with any of its Ford counterparts, apart from a Woodruff key and its sump plug!

SPECIFICATION	JAGUAR XK8
ENGINE	V-8, 3996 cc
HORSEPOWER	285 bhp @ 5800 rpm
TRANSMISSION	Automatic 5-speed
CHASSIS	Uniary steel
BRAKES	Discs all round with ABS
TOP SPEED	158 mph (254 km/h)
ACCELERATION	**0-60 mph** 6.2 seconds **0-100 mph** 16.1 seconds

LAMBORGHINI MIURA P400S

1970
172 mph
277 km/h

'The reception was fantastic and many orders were placed for the new car.'

First of the genuine production supercars, the Miura was everyone's ideal at its 1966 launch.

Lamborghini's name became world-famous on the back of the Miura. Mid-engined with a transverse V-12, and clad in beautiful Bertone bodywork, it was the ultimate road-racer which generated ecstatic acclaim when it appeared at the 1966 Geneva Show. What is also remarkable about the Lamborghini operation is that a brand new company, started in 1962, should have been able to create two new and widely diverse cars – the front-engined 350GT being the first – in the space of just four years, including designing and developing a new V-12 engine, and building and equipping a new factory.

Tractor magnate Ferruccio Lamborghini was a perfectionist who wanted to create the ideal GT car; he had tried all the others and believed he could do better. Setting up in Sant'Agata Bolognese, not far from Ferrari and Maserati, was not a gibe at the establishment; it was just a good area for getting engineering work done well and quickly as well as providing the right kind of people. A nucleus was formed around ex-Maserati people, Paolo Stanzani, Giampaolo Dallara with New Zealander Bob Wallace joining in as development engineer. The engine was designed by Giotto Bizzarrini; a 3.5-litre V-12 with twin cams per bank, the prototype gave over 350 bhp at 8000 rpm, subsequently tamed by Dallara to a still respectable 270 bhp at 6500 rpm. A new tubular chassis carried all independent wishbone suspension and the first body style came from Scaglione; shown in October 1963, it was rejected in favour of a new body from Touring which found approval at Geneva in March 1964 and production started shortly after – development had been very quick.

A year later, this became the 400GT with the V-12 now at 4-litres and 320 bhp. For 1966 a 2+2 was added. Front-engined Lamborghinis were to continue through Islero, Jarama and Espada until 1978. Meanwhile, once the GT was under way in 1964, designers were looking to produce a race-style Lamborghini even though the boss would never race; race-style meant mid-engined but the normal longitudinal layout with the gearbox behind was going to make for a very long car with a V-12. Setting the engine across the frame was not a new idea – the Mini had done it in 1959 – but the execution, with an integral gearbox just behind, was quite brilliant; the complex crankcase casting was something that could only have been conceived in that area of Italy. Like the Mini, engine and gearbox shared the same oil, although this was to change in the later SV when a limited slip differential was fitted.

For the chassis, Dallara followed the air-craft monocoque principle using a sheet steel frame incorporating the roof and with extensions to carry the front suspension and cradle the engine and rear suspension, double wishbones all-round, of course. When the rolling chassis was displayed at the Turin Show in November 1965 – once again a very quick gestation – the reception was fantastic and many orders were placed for the new car, as yet un-named and un-styled. By the Geneva Show in March 1966, this had all been rectified. Bertone had been commissioned and 25-year-old Marcello Gandini

drew up the design with perhaps a little inspiration from Bertone's other star employee, Giorgio Giugiaro; it was so right that little was to be changed during the Miura's sadly short six-year run – it was killed to make way for the Countach. And the name? Born under the sign of Taurus, hence the marque's badge, Lamborghini chose the name of a Spanish fighting bull. But at that point, there was no tooling and development hadn't even started; a rush programme saw the first production car delivered just nine months later, still a steel chassis but with aluminium bodywork. The 4-litre engine finally gave 350 bhp at 7000 rpm

Performance was all that it was expected to be with a maximum around 170 mph and Wallace had done a very good job in developing the chassis in such a short time. Inevitably there was a certain amount of further development by both customer and factory before the new derivative arrived in 1969, the P400S. The chassis was stiffened and suspension modified to cope with wider, grippier tyres and the engine uprated to 370 bhp. The final version was the 1971 SV with further engine work to produce 385 bhp and redesigned suspension around even wider rear tyres, requiring slight flaring of the bodywork. All told, 762 Miuras were built taking Lamborghini firmly into the lead in the supercar fold.

SPECIFICATION	LAMBORGHINI MIURA P400S
ENGINE	Aluminium V-12, 3929 cc
HORSEPOWER	370 bhp @ 7500 rpm
TRANSMISSION	Manual 5-speed
CHASSIS	Steel with aluminium body
BRAKES	Discs all round
TOP SPEED	172 mph
ACCELERATION	**0-60 mph** 6.7 seconds **0-100 mph** 15.1 seconds

Fish-like headlights came from the Bertone Testudo and were subsequently copied for the Porsche 928; they are still the least appealing part of the design.

LAMBORGHINI COUNTACH

1986

190 mph

306 km/h

'The Countach design started with a clean sheet of paper.'

They say that *Countach* is the dialect word used when a beautiful woman slinks into view in the Piedmont area, the home of Bertone, who styled and made the body for the prototype of the Miura's replacement. In its original uncluttered form, the new car certainly deserved a verbal wolf-whistle when it emerged for the first time on its way to the public launch at the 1971 Geneva Show. Not that it was ready for production at that time; it was 1974 before the first one was ready for sale, by which time Automobili Ferruccio Lamborghini had been sold to Swiss partners. It was to be sold again before the Countach had been finished; Chrysler took over in 1987.

Although it was a replacement for the Miura and aimed at exactly the same market, the Countach design started with a clean sheet of paper embodying all the lessons that had been learnt from that first mid-engined supercar. Where the Miura had its V-12 mounted transversely, the Countach had the same engine mounted fore and aft with the gearbox in front; having a smaller unit nearest the cockpit meant less intrusion into that space and the gear linkage run was very short and direct. Drive was taken from drop-down gears through the sump to a crown wheel and pinion

within the engine's sump casting; while this raised the overall centre of gravity, the other benefits outweighed this and the weight distribution was the same 42/58 as the Miura.

The original intention had been to give the Countach a 5-litre engine and the prototype was called the LP500 to match, but the familiar 4-litre was retained in 375 bhp form after the first prototype, and the model was renamed LP400 for production. In fact, the Countach didn't start out with great volume in mind; it was conceived as a limited run supercar to promote Lamborghini technology, so the prototype was built in a labour-intensive fashion with a welded-up space-frame and a steel body adding strength. When the enthusiastic reception showed that there was a surprising demand, the space-frame was redesigned to be very stiff in its own right, and the body was made in aluminium.

While such features as the beetle-wing doors and their inset half-windows carried through to production, the original slender purity of Gandini's lines was somewhat lost during development. Aerodynamic tests deepened the nose and lost the sill-top feature crease. The rear mounted radiators were to be fed through slats behind the side

Almost a mono-volume shape, the Gandini-designed Countach lost its purity of line with radiator scoops and wheel-arch extensions.

windows, the air exiting through grilles into the hollow behind the rear window; not only did this give inadequate air throughput, but rearward visibility required windows where the slats had been, so air was supplied from a mixture of large NACA ducts on the flanks and a box-like scoop on top and went out through slats on the wing tops. Finally the car was in production and testers could see if the performance matched the looks and the hype. Lamborghini's testers had seen over 180 mph but *Motor* put down an estimated 175 mph for the maximum with 0-100 mph in 13.1 seconds – it was fast enough for most.

Original tyre testing had been with low profile Pirelli tyres, but these were slow to get into production and the LP400 used 70% profile Michelins. Finally the low and wide P7 became available; to accommodate these, the Countach grew unsightly glassfibre wheel-arch extensions

SPECIFICATION	LAMBORGHINI COUNTACH LP5000S QV
ENGINE	Aluminium V-12, 5167 cc
HORSEPOWER	455 bhp @ 7000 rpm
TRANSMISSION	Manual 5-speed
CHASSIS	Steel frame, aluminium body
BRAKES	Discs all round
TOP SPEED	190 mph
ACCELERATION	**0-60 mph** 4.9 seconds **0-100 mph** 11.0 seconds

with the front ones blended into a chin spoiler and, with revised suspension, the P400S came out in 1978, still with the same power.

Not until 1982 did the Countach finally get its 5-litre engine, actually a 4.75-litre, but the car was labelled LP500S. Emission laws had brought this on, so there was no power increase, just a drop in the revs at which it was developed from 8000 rpm to 7000 rpm. The first performance increase came in 1985 with the engine up to 5167 cc and four-valve cylinder heads combining to produce 455 bhp, still on carburetters while the catalytic version had fuel injection and 425 bhp. Magazine top speed tests of the LP5000S QV varied between 180 and 190 mph, but the latter figure was achieved by a Lamborghini tester with a brave journalist alongside so we'll accept it as representative of what the long-reigning king of the supercars could do in its final form.

Radiator air emerges from the louvres. Wheel arches had to accommodate ever wider tyres during the near-20 years of the Countach existence.

Squat and purposeful, the final Countach 5000S QV had 455 bhp to propel it up to 190 mph.

LAMBORGHINI DIABLO SE30

1995
207 mph
333 km/h

*Lamborghini revived the SV
(Sport Veloce) name for a
lightweight version of the Diablo,
introduced in 1996. Acceleration
is better but lower gearing and
greater aerodynamic drag
meant a reduction in top speed
to 183 mph.*

Following the Countach was no easy task; it had been king of the supercars for 16 years. During that time the company had two owners which slowed progress on a replacement; however Chrysler's take-over in 1987 did much to help the Diablo on its way towards membership of the 200 mph club. Its new body shape was the work of Marcello Gandini, who had penned the original Countach during his time with Bertone. As with most designs, the Diablo was the ultimate evolution of its forerunner – retaining the same overall design, lengthened by six inches to leave space for a four-wheel-drive system.

The Countach power-train layout was ideal for four-wheel-drive; most mid-engined systems have the gearbox behind the engine, making a connection to the front wheels very difficult. The Countach put the gearbox ahead of the V-12 engine – it was a normal front-engine/gearbox swung through 180 degrees – and drove the rear wheels via step down gears and a shaft running under the engine through the sump. For the four-wheel-drive Diablo VT that transfer gear sends drive to the front wheels as well, albeit via a torque splitting centre differential.

While the Countach grew scoops and air-ducts during development, the Diablo's exterior is clean and functional, a thing of aggressive beauty, but still a single volume shape with hardly a break in profile at the base of the screen. Wind tunnel work had removed the need for a rear wing, although these are often fitted. In standard form the Lambo engine is now 5.7-litres, up from the Countach's 5.17-litre to allow cleaner emissions, but still produces 492 bhp, which is enough to power the better shape to 205 mph recorded at Nardo's test track; the VT, introduced in 1991, loses a little power through its extra transmission gears and stops at 202 mph, while extra weight robs a few tenths from the acceleration times.

Since then there have been several niche models. For 1993, the year Chrysler sold the company to Indonesian MegaTech, the Special Edition marked the 30th anniversary of

'Given the power increase, it is not surprising that the manufacturer claimed 207 mph.'

Lamborghini production; for this two-wheel-drive car a traction control system has been added to cope with a power increase to 525 bhp, and the weight has been reduced from the Diablo's 1575 Kg to 1460 Kg by strategic use of magnesium castings and carbon-fibre composites – the all-composite McLaren weighs in at 1150 Kg. Outwardly, the main differences are a mildly reshaped nose, a slatted carbon-fibre engine cover filling the hollow behind the rear window and an adjuster flap in the middle of the fitted rear wing. Given the power increase, it is not surprising that the manufacturer claimed 207 mph; the 0-100 mph time came down from the Diablo's already impressive 9.7 seconds to 9.3 seconds.

The Jota was faster still. In general, Lamborghinis have never officially raced, although the company's engineering division produced *Grand Prix* engines in the early 'nineties, but the return of interest in GT racing prompted the 1995 launch of the Jota as the racing Diablo for privateers; for this, the same 5.7-litre V-12 was further developed with variable length inlet tracts and exhaust system valves to produce an astonishing 590 bhp. Although the Jota was conceived as a racer, it could be used on the road and its uprating features would fit any SE30. A standard road-going SE30 was plenty fast enough but production was limited to that 30th anniversary year.

No one went racing with a Jota, so that model gave way to the SV (Sport Veloce) for 1996. Less extreme than the SE30, this received a 508 bhp version of the 5.7-litre, together with lower gearing for faster acceleration and more downforce from a bigger rear wing – a better track specification. The final version has been the VT-based Roadster with a Targa top, whose roof panel can be stored by straddling the valley behind the rear window; its performance will be similar to that of the hard-top Diablo VT.

SPECIFICATION	LAMBORGHINI DIABLO SE30	LAMBORGHINI DIABLO
ENGINE	Aluminium V-12, 5707 cc	Aluminium V-12, 5707 cc
HORSEPOWER	525 bhp @ 7100 rpm	492 bhp @ 7000 rpm
TRANSMISSION	Manual 5-speed	Manual 5-speed
CHASSIS	Steel frame, ali-carbon body	Steel frame, ali-carbon body
BRAKES	Discs all round	Discs all round
TOP SPEED	207 mph (333 km/h)	205 mph (330 km/h)
ACCELERATION	**0-60 mph** 4.2 seconds **0-100 mph** 9.3 seconds	4.4 seconds 9.7 seconds

LISTER STORM GTL

1997

200 mph

321 km/h

'The press speculated that it was capable of speeds approaching 240 mph.'

The Storm GTL of 1997, which retains the substructure of the original car graced with a new body. Its is claimed to increase downforce and so improve cornering. The lightened version has a similar top speed to the original.

To anyone who followed sports racing in the 1950s, mention of the Lister-Jaguar name will produce a misty eyed but, above all, positive response. Some 40 years on, in 1993, Lister was effectively reborn with the arrival of the chunky 200 mph Storm supercar and the latest version of the design, the GTL, is a head turner if ever there was one.

Although the Cambridge-based light engineering company of George Lister and Sons withdrew from competition in 1960, in 1984 it launched a club racing series for XJ-S owners. One of the entrants drove a car prepared by Laurence Pearce, son of Warren, noted Jaguar club racer of the 1960s, and, in the best traditions, it won first time out. A link was thus forged between Pearce and the Lister company.

In 1986 Pearce established W.P. Automotive in Leatherhead, Surrey to build and market modified versions of the Jaguar XJ-S coupé under the Lister Le Mans and Mark III names.

But although he undertook extensive work on the model and produced what he regarded as 'the ultimate XJ-S', Laurence Pearce recognised that any further development would require the proverbial clean sheet of paper. The eventual result was the Lister Storm, a sensational coupé powered, appropriately, by a 7-litre Jaguar-based XJ-S V-12 engine.

By February 1991 Laurence had obtained sufficient capital to begin work and, from the outset, he was aiming to produce a design that embodied what he called the 'front-mid-engined concept.'

As such the power unit was mounted as far back in the monocoque as practical. Such a location meant that four occupants could be accommodated and there was no noisy intrusive mid-located engine that is a feature of the overwhelming majority of supercars.

Attention was also paid to the car's underside which was flat so that it could benefit from the 'ground effect' developed for racing cars to achieve the most efficient roadholding.

Two-door coupé bodywork, that stylistically resembled a mid-engined model, was the work of Mike Hughes. It was made mostly of carbon-fibre with aluminium-faced steel doors which cloaked a chassis constructed of honeycomb-sandwich aluminium alloy and Kevlar. The drag coefficient was a respectable 0.32.

The Storm, the product of Pearce's Lister Cars, certainly made waves when it was unveiled at the 1993 London Motor Show. Costing no less than £219,725, the press speculated that it was capable of speeds approaching 240 mph although the true figure was probably nearer the 195 mark.

Having said that, no magazine has tested the Storm flat out although *Autocar* recorded a 0 to 60 mph time of 4.7 seconds whilst 0 to 100 mph was achieved in a mere 11 seconds.

Such performance was only possible because the output of the engine, which in its original 6-litre form developed 308 bhp, was upped to a

SPECIFICATION	LISTER STORM GTL
ENGINE	Aluminium V-12, 6996 cc
HORSEPOWER	450 bhp @ 6100 rpm
TRANSMISSION	Manual 6-speed
CHASSIS	Aluminium honeycomb
BRAKES	Discs all round with ABS
TOP SPEED	200 mph plus (321 km/h)
ACCELERATION	**0-60 mph** 4 seconds **0-100 mph** 8 seconds

formidable 594. It comes as little surprise to find that only the Jaguar block and cylinder heads were retained, the remainder of parts were unique to the Storm.

The increase in capacity, to 7-litres, was achieved by increasing the engine's bore and stroke which required the use of Cosworth cylinder liners and pistons and a purpose-created crankshaft. Flowed cylinder heads, reprofiled camshafts, revised inlet system and, above all, two belt-driven radial superchargers, blowing at 10 psi, did the rest.

The respected Ricardo engineering consultancy was responsible for analysing the engine's porting and combustion systems and advised on the emissions and catalytic legislation.

A six-speed Getrag gearbox was attached directly to the engine and drive conveyed, via a stubby propeller shaft, to a ZF differential.

The well appointed, leather-trimmed interior was enhanced by the fitment of purpose built air conditioning whilst the Kenwood stereo system was also made especially for the Storm. The power assisted steering operated at just two-and-a-half turns lock to lock.

Since its announcement, some 20 Storms have been sold and Lister ran an example at Le Mans in 1995. This unsupercharged car, with output boosted to 640 bhp, touched 202 mph down the Mulsanne Straight. Subsequently, in the 1996 event, one of these distinctive coupés finished in a creditable 19th position, despite experiencing engine problems on the last lap.

Now the concept has evolved and the result is the rebodied Storm GTL (for Lightweight) which appeared in the spring of 1997, that retains the essentials of the Storm's substructure. Although the V-12 has been shorn of its superchargers, engine efficiency has been boosted so that output remains the same at 594 bhp.

Bodywork, essayed by Geoff Kingston, aims to increase downforce and so improve the car's cornering. The weight saving is significant for, at 1150 kg, the GTL is 288 kg lighter than its predecessor. Distinctive body features are the fins ahead of the front wheels to improve brake cooling, while a similar function is performed by vents mounted ahead of the rear wheels.

At the time of writing the GTL had not been road tested by a motoring magazine but Lister claim a 200 mph top speed, with 60 mph coming up in a mere four seconds and 100 mph whistling by in just eight.

Orders have already been taken for five cars and, as in the past, Lister has set its sights on Le Mans. Drivers Tiff Needell and Geoff Lees have been signed to drive in the 1997 GT racing season although competition from both Porsche and McLaren is formidable. What is not is dispute is that the GTL is going to be well worth watching.

The original Lister Storm, a front-engined supercar with a claimed top speed of 200 mph. As such, four people could be accommodated. Powered by a supercharged Jaguar-based V-12 engine, it has now been succeeded by the GTL version.

The Storm's supercharged 7-litre, Jaguar-based, V-12 engine sat well back in the chassis. Its internals were specially designed for the model and output was a massive 450 bhp. This was conveyed via a six-speed Getrag gearbox.

LOTUS ESPRIT V8

1996

172 mph

277 km/h

'The Esprit has managed to retain its driver appeal.'

There is remarkably little externally to indicate the presence of the V-8 engine although the Esprit's front valance is new! Brakes and air conditioning have also been improved.

At last, Britain's only affordable mid-engined supercar has gained the power unit it has so long deserved. Lotus have designed an all-new 3.5-litre V-8 producing 350 bhp in unstressed twin-turbo form. Ultra-compact, it slots into the tail of the Esprit with no difficulty and will push the top speed up to over 170 mph, while the extra torque will make the car even faster off the line.

The major reason for the new unit was that the turbo-four was no longer acceptable for American emissions legislation. However the investment in a new engine will not be recovered solely on Lotus production volumes, so expect to see others using it. Meanwhile, the 2.2-litre S4 series will continue to be available in the short term, with the recall of the 2-litre turbo adding an entry-level GT3 to the range.

Although the design concept of the Lotus Esprit is still that of the 1972 Turin Show car, it has undergone so many developments in every area that almost nothing physical remains of the original; it still has a backbone chassis carrying a mid-mounted engine in a striking body with a similar silhouette, but that is about it. Its origins go back before 1972. Lotus had used their twin-cam

version of the Ford engine for the Elan and the Europa Twin-Cam, but the engine was not going to meet the stricter emission regulations of the mid-'seventies. The new engine for the next generation of cars was based on the 2-litre Vauxhall slant-four; with a Lotus 16-valve head, this LV220 would power the new Elite, Eclat and Esprit range. Progress on the new cars was slow, so the engine first saw production service in the Jensen Healey from 1972.

Meanwhile Lotus' founder, Colin Chapman, had let ItalDesign have a prototype mid-engined chassis in 1971; when the resultant Esprit was highly praised at the 1972 Turin Show, Chapman pushed the design through as fast as possible alongside the two front-engined cars. All would use a backbone chassis, of the type used on the Elan or Europa, with glass-fibre bodies built on Lotus' patent Vacuum Assisted Resin Injection process. While the front-engined cars retained the Elan's later 5-speed box, the Esprit borrowed the Citroen transaxle that had been built for the SM and the Maserati Merak. The 4-seater hatch-back Lotus Elite finally came in mid-1974, with the cheaper fast-back Eclat and the mid-engined Esprit

following in October 1975; tooling delays then deferred the Esprit's production start until mid-1976.

With 160 bhp, the Esprit was capable of 135 mph, a considerable improvement over the 105 bhp Europa Twin-Cam's 117 mph. An S2 version arrived for 1978 with minor cosmetic changes and a torquier camshaft, but the major change was to come in 1980 with the arrival of the Turbo and engine capacity increased to 2.2-litres, a size which had been developed for the Sunbeam-Lotus and was to span the Lotus range. Body changes saw a full-width chin spoiler blending into side-skirts and a rear spoiler denoting the 210 bhp Turbo, the first 100 of which were sold in the racing Essex Lotus colours – suspension changes adjusted to the wider wheels. The new maximum was near 150 mph.

The next major change came with the subtle, but effective, 1987 restyle by Peter Stevens; Giugiaro's original origami creases were smoothly rounded while front and rear bumpers were integrated to give a much more modern appearance. By now the power was up to 218 bhp, with the US version using fuel injection for the same figure.

The 1989 model year saw non-turbo units phased out as fuel injection versions were increased to 231 bhp, but the Special Equipment model used higher boost pressure with an intercooler to generate 268 bhp and had a rear wing to prove it; this became the S4 in 1993. Meanwhile Birmingham 1992 had seen the Sport 300 with a bigger turbocharger, stiffer suspension and fatter wheels. Two years later the S4S arrived with a slightly smaller turbo to give better low down response at the expense of a minor power drop to 285 bhp; a clever compromise, it retained most of the 300's race-proven roadholding but with the S4's comfort.

With some 20 years of steady refinement behind it, the Esprit has managed to retain its driver appeal despite the lack of engine sophistication. With its new, more powerful and much quieter V-8, the latest Esprit will please a much wider market.

The presence of the new V-8 is more apparent from the car's rear with a badge on the back panel and twin exhaust pipes as the give-aways. Inside there's a V8 motif on the rev counter . . .

Installed longitudinally, the twin turbocharged 3.5-litre aluminium V-8 was created in a little over two years and although it develops 350 bhp it seems likely that there's plenty in reserve for enlargements in capacity.

SPECIFICATION	LOTUS ESPRIT V8
ENGINE	Twin-turbo V-8, 3506 cc
HORSEPOWER	350 bhp @ 6250 rpm
TRANSMISSION	Manual 5-speed
CHASSIS	Steel backbone
BRAKES	Discs all round with ABS
TOP SPEED	172 mph (277 km/h)
ACCELERATION	**0-60 mph** 4.5 seconds **0-100 mph** 11.3 seconds

MARCOS MANTIS

1997
170 mph
274 km/h

Marcos is one of the handful of car companies that continues to constitute the British-owned motor industry. The 1997 Mantis, that revives a corporate model name, is a distinctive and potent two-seater capable of speeds approaching the 170 mph mark.

The Marcos make dates from 1959 and is so called because its founders, Jem Marsh and Frank Costin, allotted the first three letters of their respective surnames to the company. Racing driver Marsh contributed an all-important competition ingredient which the marque still maintains.

Frank Costin, with an aviation background, was an aerodynamicist of note who had essayed the lines of the Formula 1 Vanwall, and was responsible for the Marcos' ungainly but windcheating silhouette and its unique light and robust wooden chassis. Power came from a variety of Ford engines.

Costin left the firm in 1961, at which point brothers Dennis and Peter Adams took over development. In 1963 came a move to Bradford on Avon, Wiltshire and, later the same year, the arrival of the 115 mph Volvo-powered 1800, a low and distinctive glass-fibre coupé, styled by Dennis Adams. Originally intended as a stop gap measure, and also available as a kit car, its timeless lines form the inspiration for the current Marcos range.

Later, in 1969, the idiosyncratic, but labour intensive, marine ply chassis was dispensed with and was replaced by a more conventional square tubular spaceframe which reduced the overall manufacturing process by a substantial 15 hours.

The company had, in 1966, introduced the Mini Marcos coupé, a stumpy glass-fibre bodied kit car, to which the buyer contributed Mini or Mini Cooper mechanicals. Creditably an example entered for that year's Le Mans event finished 15th and was the only British car to complete the race.

In 1970 Marcos unveiled the Triumph TR6-engined Mantis, a controversially styled two-plus-two-seater coupé which failed to catch on – just 33 were built. Soon afterwards, in 1972, a combination of circumstances, including a move to new premises at nearby Westbury, forced the firm's closure.

Jem Marsh, however, continued to supply owners with spare parts. In 1976 he re-acquired the Marcos name and body moulds and in 1981 revived the Adams-styled coupé, now dubbed the 3-litre on account of its Ford V-6 power unit. In

SPECIFICATION	MARCOS MANTIS
ENGINE	Aluminium V-8, 4601 cc
HORSEPOWER	352 bhp @ 6000 rpm
TRANSMISSION	Manual 5-speed
CHASSIS	Square section tubular steel
BRAKES	Discs all round with ABS
TOP SPEED	Around 170 mph (274 km/h)
ACCELERATION	**0-60 mph** 4.1 seconds **0-100 mph** – no figures available

The Mantis' aerodynamically refined body looks both back and forwards, to the classic 1960s shape but also reflects the company's experience on the race track with its GT car. The tubular steel spaceframe chassis has similarly benefited from competition. Power is courtesy of Ford America's twin cam V-8, also used in the Mustang, tweaked to produce 352 bhp.

1984 it was revised as the Mantula with a 3.5-litre Rover V-8 engine and from 1986 was also built in Spyder (open) form with Ford-based independent rear suspension following three years later.

The present generation of Marcos dates from the revised Mantara of 1993 which perpetuated the closed and open options. On this model the original Triumph Herald front suspension was replaced by Ford Sierra-sourced MacPherson struts and attendant rack and pinion steering gear. This necessitated revisions to the chassis and body panels and the introduction of flared wheel arches front and rear.

Produced in 3.9-litre 400 and uprated 4.5-litre 450 forms, the company claimed that the latter had a top speed in excess of 150 mph with 0 to 60 mph spirited up in just 4.7 seconds.

This model was the first in which Jem Marsh's son, Chris had an involvement having returned from America after a successful career there as a crew chief and test driver.

Marcos unveiled the Mantara's Le Mans racing derivative at the 1993 London Motor Show with a new (although clearly related) coupé body designed, once again, by Dennis Adams. Powered by an enlarged 5-litre V-8 engine, and intended for use on both road and track, the LM, as it subsequently became, was followed in 1995 by the supplementary LM600 with a 6.1-litre Chevrolet V-8.

This brought Team Marcos the 1995 UK GT title in the hands of Chris Hodgetts. The 600 is now actively campaigning in GT events the world over.

In 1995 Marcos returned to Le Mans, which it had last entered in 1967, when an LM 600 driven by Cor Euser and Tommy Erdos, succeeded in finishing the 24 hour race.

The following year's British Motor Show saw the announcement of the Mantis powered by Ford's 4.6-litre V-8, with twin overhead-camshafts per cylinder bank, courtesy of its Mustang Cobra, where it developed 310 bhp. But ministrations by the still Westbury-based Marcos team pushed this figure up to 352 bhp. These have taken the form of a new exhaust layout and revised engine management system.

The glass-fibre composite body, styled by Leigh Adams, draws on Marcos' experience on the circuits with its Chevrolet-engined GT racers whilst the spaceframe chassis has similarly benefited.

A prospective Marcos owner usually chooses his or her own interior, in which seats can be upholstered in leather that complements a veneered dashboard of natural elm. Air conditioning and power steering are standard fitments. The Mantis is priced at almost £44,000 and there are a host of extra goodies available.

The spring of 1997 saw the appearance of the S Mantis, an even more exciting 452bhp supercharged version which, says Marcos, is capable of 184 mph . . .

Although this is the Spyder (open) version, the Mantis is also available in coupé form. The distinctive lines, the work of Leigh Adams, have been refined in a wind tunnel for low drag. As a result the shape generates downforce that aids high speed handling and safety. Like all Marcos cars, the model is handbuilt by a small team of craftsman at the firm's Wiltshire factory. Advanced projector lighting is featured.

'Seats can be upholstered in leather that complements a veneered dashboard of natural elm.'

MASERATI BORA

1973
160 mph
257 km/h

'Finding reliable Maserati top speed figures is still difficult.'

With a race-bred 4.7-litre V-8 turning out some 310 bhp, the mid-engined Bora was a sensational car when it was first shown in 1971. Although there were faster front-engined cars, only the Lamborghini Miura was in the same mid-engined ball-park. The specification was interesting enough, but the body had been designed by Giugiaro at the height of his classical period, when sports cars were designed, and often built, by coachbuilders, and practical family ware had only just begun to show styling influence; the Bora – a strong wind – suggested the coiled energy of a greyhound poised to leave the trap. Nearly 500 would leave the Modena factory over the next seven years, the later ones with 4.9-litre engines.

Finding reliable Maserati top speed figures is still difficult; the factory claims were never accurate and speedometers even less so. *Motor's* 1973 test estimated 160 mph, others believed the factory 168 mph at 6000 rpm; but acceleration figures were taken and were usually slightly better than those for the Miura. It was certainly a fast car and reasonably practical for touring with a good-sized front boot but detail failings let it down in the eyes of period observers – poor heating and ventilation, inadequate room for tall drivers and less for passengers – but its drivability was always highly rated.

The Bora was a product of the Citroen period of ownership from 1969-75; although most of the design was pure Maserati, including the traditional tubular frame, there was some Citroen influence, notably in the power braking system. More obviously Citroen-inspired was the Merak which arrived a year and a half later; this shared most of the Bora's chassis and bodywork with a different rear deck treatment but was powered by an enlarged version of the four-cam V-6 which

Comprehensive instrumentation is provided in the Bora. The brake pedal is part of a Citroen system and thus has almost zero travel.

Maserati had designed for the Citroen SM – the SM had 170 bhp from 2670 cc, the Merak 190 bhp from 2965 cc. As the V-6 with a Citroen gearbox was somewhat shorter than the V-8 installation, Maserati fitted a pair of small rear seats within the same wheelbase, so the Merak was a little more practical but slower with a 140 mph maximum.

Citroen retreated from Modena in 1975 and Maserati was taken over by de Tomaso. While Merak SS (220 bhp), with the Khamsin and Quattroporte, were to continue in production into the 'eighties, De Tomaso was changing the company's direction to capitalise on the name with greater volume; the result was launched in 1982 as the Biturbo, a 2-door sports-saloon with a 2-litre V-6 using three valves per cylinder and twin-turboed to produce 180 bhp. Italian taxes favour 2-litre units, so it pays to get the best from that size. Technically it was worthy of the Maserati name, but the style was uninspiring. Subsequent model names juggled with numbers of doors and engine sizes on varying wheelbases to produce 228,

425, 430 with a short-wheelbase open Spyder having appeared in 1984.

In 1990 names came back and the Shamal was introduced with a new 32-valve 3.2-litre V-8 still with twin turbos to produce 325 bhp within a hardtop version of the short spyder; with bulging flanks to cover wide wheels, the old Biturbo shape has taken on a new lease of life. It's quick, too, with a six-speed Getrag gearbox to help; 0-100 mph should come up in under 13 seconds. The Ghibli name was brought back in 1992 for the normal 2-door model to be fitted with either the 284 bhp 2.8-litre V-6 or the Italian special 2-litre boosted to 306 bhp, both forms capable of over 150 mph. The following year saw Fiat take over from de Tomaso, hopefully to ensure that the historic name continues to be attached to the fast sporting cars that were its life-blood for so long.

SPECIFICATION	MASERATI BORA
ENGINE	Aluminium V-8, 4719 cc
HORSEPOWER	310 bhp @ 6000 rpm
TRANSMISSION	Manual 5-speed
CHASSIS	Steel frame and body
BRAKES	Discs all round
TOP SPEED	160 mph
ACCELERATION	**0-60 mph** 6.5 seconds **0-100 mph** 14.7 seconds

Large rear window gives some rearward visibility; but there is a surprising amount of luggage space available in the front.

Styled by Giugiaro from his own company, ItalDesign, the Bora looks coiled and ready to go.

McLaren F1

1993

231 mph

372 km/h

'It is geared to reach 'only' 220 mph.'

This is the limited edition LM (for Le Mans) version of the F1, note the initials on the sill ahead of the rear wheel. It used the revised front and wing of the GTR track car to improve downforce. The Peter Stevens-styled body imbues the car with a sense of movement even when stationary.

It was August 8, 1993 at the Nardo test track in southern Italy. McLaren's tester, former *Grand Prix* driver Jonathan Palmer, was doing routine high-speed testing with prototype XP3. On the last outing of the day, he kept his foot flat over the whole of a standing start lap of the 7.8-mile banked circuit; for two heady miles it clocked 231 mph. It was the fastest ever recorded for a road-going car, faster even than the racing McLarens were going to achieve.

Although its design is full of *Grand Prix* technology and the name has been synonymous with *Grand Prix* success, the McLaren F1 was not created to go racing; it was just meant to be the ultimate road car of *Grand Prix* car designer, Gordon Murray. Lightweight carbon-fibre chassis and bodywork, sophisticated shock-absorbing suspension sub-frames, race-style 1+2 seating, transverse 6-speed gearbox and a purpose built 6.1-litre BMW V-12 engine were just a few of the design highlights.

While the McLaren was in the latter stages of development, the FIA's World Sports Car championship had fallen on difficult times and the regulations were heading towards production GT racing, hoping to bring all those supercars to the tracks. Being the newest, and the most race-orientated in its design, the F1 suddenly seemed the ideal car for the new championship.

Launched on the downside of the supercar boom in May 1992, the McLaren F1 had not had an easy time. The plan had been to make 350 at a rate of four cars per month, selling at £530,000 plus taxes. By the time the first car was delivered in January 1994, 350 seemed an impossible target in a vanishing market and it was only possible to build three cars a month. Despite the avowed intention not to go racing with the F1, McLaren could not pass up the opportunity to give the car its own track record and create a few more cars.

The 1994 production numbers were sufficient to homologate the car for racing, so McLaren needed little persuasion to engineer a competition version. Good though the F1 was for road use, it didn't need shock-absorbing rubber in its engine mounts or suspension sub-frames, and it certainly didn't need the weight of air-conditioning or the hi-fi system. It also needed more downforce and a stronger gearbox for track use. So the changes were considerable, but seven GTRs were built in time for the 1995 racing season; they ran away with the Global GT Endurance Series, and won the Le Mans 24-hours at the first attempt.

To celebrate five Le Mans finishers (1st, 3rd,

4th, 5th, 13th), McLaren produced a limited edition of just five F1 LMs, road-going versions of the GTR, and finished in the old McLaren orange from the days when Bruce McLaren and Denny Hulme dominated Can-Am racing. The standard F1 produced 627 bhp, the 1995 GTR with regulation restrictors gave 636 bhp, but the unrestricted LM has 668 bhp to play with; however, like the GTR it generates significant downforce which increases the aerodynamic drag and it is geared to reach 'only' 220 mph. In theory, with a more free-revving power unit and closer ratio gears, it should accelerate even faster than the F1; that reaches 100 mph in just 6.3 seconds while in third gear. The LM will reach the same speed in second gear, so 5.9 seconds is entirely believable. As both will reach 60 mph in 1st gear, the improvement is nominal.

The LM is likely to remain the most accelerative of the F1s as the 1996 GT regulations asked for even more restriction in a bid to equalise the power outputs of the contenders. The 1996 GTR develops a 'mere' 600 bhp, but many other changes ensured it was even faster around the circuits; eight of those have been built.

Maybe the F1 wasn't planned as a racer, but racing success has given it the credibility it had never quite achieved as just a road-going supercar. F1 production is being stopped before even 100

have been built; without the racing versions, it would have been 20 fewer. It may not have been a financial success but it has been a superb flagship for McLaren's engineering ability.

A 1994 F1 pictured outside the firm's factory in Woking, Surrey. Unusually the steering wheel is in the centre of the cockpit.

SPECIFICATION	McLAREN F1	McLAREN F1 LM
ENGINE	Aluminium V-12 6064 cc	Aluminium V-12 6064 cc
HORSEPOWER	627 bhp @ 7400 rpm	668 bhp @ 7800 rpm
TRANSMISSION	Manual 6-speed, transverse	Manual 6-speed, transverse
CHASSIS	Carbon-fibre composite	Carbon-fibre composite
BRAKES	Discs all round	Discs all round
TOP SPEED	231 mph (372 km/h)	220 mph (354 km/h)
ACCELERATION	**0-60 mph** 3.2 seconds **0-100 mph** 6.3 seconds	3.0 seconds 5.9 seconds

MERCEDES-BENZ 600SL

1992

168 mph
(see text)

270 km/h

'It is rare to see a Mercedes listed among the fastest production cars.'

The latest generation of SL are technical marvels; they include a roll-bar that erects automatically if roll-over is imminent.

Ever since Mercedes returned to racing in 1952 and won Le Mans with the 300SL coupé, SL (Sport Light) has denoted the sporting Mercedes. Then, as now, type numbers refer to the capacity minus a zero. That first racer used all the mechanical components of the 300-series announced a year earlier, but fitted them into a new space-frame chassis with an aerodynamic body featuring gull-wing doors. Under pressure from the American importer, the factory then developed a production equivalent, still with a space-frame chassis, which was announced in early 1954. It was the supercar of its day with 150 mph performance given the highest optional ratio; with the standard ratio the maximum was 140 mph with 0-60 mph in 7.0 sec and 0-100 mph in 16.2 seconds – amazing figures for 1954. Alongside it came the smaller engined 190SL, and the Roadster 300SL came in 1957 to replace the coupé; both were phased out in 1963 to make way for the new 230SL, no longer a road-going racer but a short wheelbase, higher powered derivative of the saloon range, the pattern of years to come – future SLs would be neither Sport nor Light until the arrival of the little SLK.

The 230/250/280SL series, with six-cylinder engines, ran through to 1971. Although 280 and 300SL models would arrive with six-cylinder engines, the new range was mostly V-8 powered from 3.5 litre 350SL to the American market 5.6-litre 560SL and also included longer 2+2 versions as 350 and 450SLC. The latest series started in 1989 with a 300SL six as well as the V-8 500SL; since then, the sixes are split into two models, 280 and 320, with a 6-litre V-12 as the flagship arriving in 1992 – now an SL600 as Mercedes decided to put the class before the capacity in 1994. These are wonderful pieces of engineering for fast comfortable travel in style; the roll-over bar which pops up in the event of an accident is just one example of the design sophistication. The body shape is also very good aerodynamically with a drag factor of 0.31, but this is more for fuel economy than sheer speed.

It is rare to see a Mercedes listed among the fastest production cars, particularly since they, along with BMW, have decided to limit top speeds electronically to 250 km/h (155 mph); however, sometimes the limiter allows a little more and *Autocar* clocked the the 600SL and the 600SEL at

159 mph. At Mercedes, outright performance is less important than longevity, so the engines have always been relatively unstressed with low bhp/litre figures and maximum speeds have not been as high as the equivalent model BMWs of unlimited days. Even if the limiter is deleted, the cars are unlikely to go much faster as the gearing is now generally chosen for the engine to peak near 250 km/h, which is better for acceleration.

Working out how fast they should go isn't difficult if you start with the 230 bhp SL320 which has been timed at a non-limited 144 mph. Give the same car the 5-litre V-8 with 320 bhp and the theoretical maximum goes to 162 mph. Use the 6-litre V-12 with 394 bhp and theory gives 174 mph which, on present gearing, would ask the engine to do over 6000 rpm. For comparison's sake we have settled for 168 mph as a true indication of the SL600's potential without artificial restriction. The

SL500 would be slower in top speed but actually returns very similar acceleration figures as the V-12 version is 10 percent (180 Kg) heavier than the V-8; it is also rather more than 10 percent thirstier in the standard EEC tests. Since both SL500 and SL600 are limited to the same maximum speed and the smaller version is more economical and faster off the mark, why have an SL600? Simply because it represents the pinnacle of Mercedes technology; they may not make the fastest cars in the world but there is nothing finer than the ultimate in Mercedes engineering.

Mercedes' governors limit the 600SEL to the same top speed as the SL but the big 4-door is little slower in acceleration taking 15.8 seconds from 0-100 mph.

The big V-12 adds a lot of weight to the SL but offers the ultimate refinement.

SPECIFICATION	MERCEDES-BENZ 600SL
ENGINE	Aluminium V-12, 5987 cc
HORSEPOWER	394 bhp @ 5200 rpm
TRANSMISSION	Auto 5-speed
CHASSIS	Unitary steel
BRAKES	Discs all round with ABS
TOP SPEED	168 mph
ACCELERATION	**0-60 mph** 6.0 seconds **0-100 mph** 14.4 seconds

MERCEDES-BENZ CLK-GTR

1997
200+ mph
321+ km/h

'The CLK-GTR weighs 1200 kg, and is expected to be capable of reaching 60 mph in a mere 3.5 seconds and have a top speed in excess of the magic 200 mph.'

Mercedes-Benz, with a racing pedigree that reaches back to the dawn of motoring, has produced a sensational 200 mph roadgoing version of the sports racer it intends to campaign in GT events during the 1997 season.

This is a series that attracts the likes of the Porsche GT1 and the McLaren F1 GTR and the new road car is intended to help Mercedes-Benz shed its refined but rather staid image.

It is hoped that the CLK-GTR will do wonders for the company's appeal among the younger generation of potential purchasers. That is certainly the hope of Jurgen Schrempp, chairman of the firm's Daimler-Benz parent, who is intent on endowing Mercedes-Benz with an enhanced, performance-honed profile.

The silver-hued coupé, for which the company has revived the traditional but unofficial Silver Arrow designation, has been developed in conjunction with its Stuttgart-based AMG tuning partner.

The distinctive gull-wing doors are in the spirit of Mercedes-Benz' legendary 300SL coupé of the 1950s. That model featured them because of

an innovative spaceframe chassis although this latter-day version has a carbon-fibre hull. Its lines are loosely based on those of the company's new CLK coupé, introduced in the summer of 1997, and aimed foursquare at a market dominated by BMW's Series 3 coupé.

The four distinctive, slightly reclining oval headlights were first seen on a concept coupé that, to the surprise of many, Mercedes-Benz unveiled at the 1993 Geneva Motor Show.

This was the first outward manifestation of the company adopting a more distinctive appearance to its magnificently engineered products. The new nose, complete with the traditional Mercedes-Benz radiator daringly inclined, made its production debut on the new E-class cars of 1995.

The company has made great play of the fact that the contours of its nose closely resemble those of its famous 1950s sports racing SLR roadster, so underlining its competition pedigree.

These features were subsequently adopted in essence, if not detail, for the smaller CLK coupé but despite their use on the sensational racer

If appearance is anything to go by, this Mercedes-Benz should be a formidable performer on both road and track. This is the roadgoing version based on the new CLK coupé although only the radiator and lights are related. It is thought that about 50 will be produced over the next two years.

tamed for road use, this car was otherwise mechanically unrelated to it.

For while the CLK is powered by a choice of front-mounted, four-cylinder unit or the new V-6 engine, on the GTR power comes from a mid-located, longitudinally-mounted V-12 which, in essence, first appeared in the company's commodious S-Class range introduced in 1991.

This 90 degree V unit, with twin overhead-camshafts per cylinder bank and four valves per cylinder, in 6-litre form developed 389 bhp. But for this stunning two-seater, complete with obligatory rear wing, the engine is enlarged to 6.9-litre and develops no less than 560 bhp.

This has been created with input from the British Ilmor Engineering of Brixworth, Northants, a firm that designs and builds racing engines, in which Mercedes-Benz has a financial interest. It is responsible for the V-10 unit that powers the current Formula 1 McLaren-Mercedes racer.

In the GTR it is attached directly to the composite hull and thus has a supporting role. Drive is taken via a six-speed sequential gearbox and the rose-jointed coil and wishbones suspension is bolted directly to it. Dampers are adjustable and the wheels substantial 18-inch diameter units.

These mechanicals are cloaked with an impressive Kevlar coupé body which retains the familiar Mercedes-Benz oblong radiator grille and even features the marque's famous tristar mascot.

The cockpit comes complete with an integrated roll cage and is surrounded by energy-absorbing, so called, crash boxes. Both driver's and co-driver's airbags are also fitted, so underlining the car's safety qualities.

The CLK-GTR weighs 1200 kg, and is expected to be capable of reaching 60 mph in a mere 3.5 seconds and have a top speed in excess of the magic 200 mph.

While Mercedes-Benz is only required under the GT racing rules to produce one example of the CLK-GTR road car, it seems likely that a limited number will be built. Produced over a two-year period for a handful of lucky owners, a figure of 50 is believed to be the most likely estimate. The cost is thought to be well below the $1 million price ceiling laid down by the FIA.

The racing version was tested by Bernd Schneider, the 1995 German Touring Car Champion and, as a result, the car made its competition debut at the first round of the GT championship at Hockenheim in April. But despite being on pole position, reliability problems resulted in it finishing in only 27th place. Nevertheless, these are early days and Le Mans beckons . . .

The CLK-GTR has been developed by the factory in conjunction with its Stuttgart-based AMG tuning partner, hence the initials on the tail. The car's longitudinally-mounted V-12 engine is bolted directly to the carbon-fibre hull. A number of passive safety features are built into the design.

SPECIFICATION	MERCEDES-BENZ CLK-GTR
ENGINE	Aluminium V-12, 6.9 litres
HORSEPOWER	560 bhp @ 7000 rpm
TRANSMISSION	Sequential 6-speed
CHASSIS	Carbon-fibre
BRAKES	Discs all round
TOP SPEED	Over 200 mph (321 km/h)
ACCELERATION	**0-60 mph** 3.5 seconds **0-100 mph** Not available

PORSCHE 959

1985
197 mph
(317 km/h)

'Tests show a maximum around 200 mph, but a 0-60 mph time of under 4 seconds.'

Loosely based on the faithful 911, the 959 is Porsche's fastest road car yet and, like so many of the Zuffenhausen projects, it was conceived with competition in mind; since Porsche regard competition as a valuable proving ground for road car technology, this was also to prove a mobile test-bed. The 959's four-wheel-drive transmission system has already been carried through to the 911 Carrera 4 and the latest Turbo 4.

Four wheel drive had existed in the Porsche design archives for many years; before and after the war, 4WD derivatives of the Beetle had been built for military use and the post-war Cisitalia GP car had four driven wheels. In the mid-'sixties, Porsche had acquired a Jensen FF to study the pros and cons of four-wheel-drive for road cars. Then their close association with Audi brought them into contact with the Quattro system prior to its 1980 launch. Porsche's first public show of 4WD interest was to present a 911 Cabriolet with 4WD as a design study in 1981. Two years later the 959 was presented as a Group B study.

Group B was the competition category for low volume production GT cars or highly modified saloons and 200 had to be made. In the early 'eighties, it was the Formula for International rallying where Audi and the Lancia Stratos were making the running; Porsche thought they would join in. They were winning most of the sports-car races (Group C) with the 956, privateers were winning Group B classes with 911 variants, and the company didn't want to go into *Grand Prix* racing, so rallying was the next challenge. The 911 had been a familiar and successful sight in 'sixties rallying, but specialism had marched on since then and four wheel drive had become essential for the loose surfaces used.

With most front-wheel drive cars the gearbox is either under a longitudinal engine or at the end of a transverse one – driving the other axle requires considerable redesign. The Audi was alone in putting the engine ahead of the front wheels, so that a normal gearbox behind it could still drive the front wheels; the Porsche 911 layout was a reversal of the same – the engine was outside

the wheelbase. For both it was relatively easy to provide drive to the other axle and both needed it, as their basic design is fundamentally wrong for safe, easy handling; the success of both has always been a triumph of development over design. Where the 959's system stood apart from all other 4WD systems was in how it allocated the driving effort between front and rear axles; all have some control system, but the 959 used a multitude of sensors to feed a computer which took the decision, or it could be over-ridden by the driver.

The 959's chassis was basically that of a 911 but the bodywork was mostly in Kevlar composites to keep the weight down. Considerable wind tunnel study had created a shape that was fundamentally 911 but which produced aerodynamic downforce. The engine was still a flat-6 but owed more to the Group C racing programme, which also provided the massive disc brakes. The engine was a 2.85-litre unit with twin turbo-chargers operating sequentially to cut down

the turbo lag – the time required for the turbos to spin up to the right speed; this produced 450 bhp with plenty of low-down pulling power. The resultant performance figures are dramatic; various tests show a maximum around 200 mph, but a 0-60 mph time of under 4 seconds.

In fact the 959 wasn't able to take the rally world by storm as the regulations had changed again by the time that the 200 had been completed in 1988. However, a 959 prototype – 4WD without turbos – won the very tough Paris-Dakar rally in 1984, and a full 959 won it in 1986; so the systems were vindicated. The 156 mph Carrera 4 adopted the 4WD, while the new Turbo has the 4WD and twin turbos on its 408 bhp 3.6-litre engine; ten years on and the 959's supercar performance for 200 lucky owners is now more readily available as just another production model.

The 911 for Group B rallying retained its factory 959 number and had some success in long-distance raids.

SPECIFICATION	PORSCHE 959
ENGINE	Aluminium flat-6 twin turbo 2850 cc
POWER	450 bhp @ 6500 rpm
TRANSMISSION	Manual 6-speed 4-wheel-drive
CHASSIS	Steel monocoque, Kevlar bodywork
BRAKES	Discs all round with ABS
TOP SPEED	197 mph (317 km/h)
ACCELERATION	**0-60 mph** 3.7 seconds **0-100 mph** 8.5 seconds

PORSCHE 928 GTS

1992
168 mph
(270 km/h)

'Rounded and almost aggressively graceful it was also good aerodynamically.'

Perhaps it is because all Porsches set out with a long model life ahead of them that the first models are not always impressive performers; they need something in hand to allow a steady increase of power during the years to come alongside the inevitable increase in technical sophistication and to offset the extra weight that comes with it. Over 15 years, the 2+2 928 has gradually changed from a 260 bhp 140 mph fast tourer to a 350 bhp 168 mph sports coupé with supercar performance; instead of being part of the high performance herd, it is now a class leader with no loss of usability on the way. It is still a very practical car that can be guaranteed to keep going for many thousands of trouble-free miles like any other Porsche – a standard setter for cars like the Aston Martin DB7.

The 928 story goes back as far as 1971. Amazingly, with hindsight, it was conceived as a replacement for the 911 which was never expected to have a model life of over 30 years. Where the 911 was really a sports car with a fairly narrow cabin and nominal space for two children in the rear, the 928 would be a spacious grand tourer in a different market sector within which driving skills could not be taken for granted; hence it would be front-engined but with handling that would still satisfy the sporting driver. The engine would be an entirely new V-8, a configuration with which the American market would feel comfortable; with 260 bhp from a single overhead camshaft design of 4.5-litres, it was not particularly stressed.

But it was to be 1977 before the car was launched, as other factors intervened. First, the 1973 oil crisis made many manufacturers think twice about big-engined cars. Secondly, VW-Audi decided not to go ahead with the little sports car which Porsche had been developing for them around many VW parts; Porsche took over the project themselves and launched the resultant 924 in 1975. By the time this was under

way, the world had again become receptive to the larger cars, so work on the 928 was resumed. Styled by American Tony Lapine, it followed the family line set for the new front-engined cars; rounded and almost aggressively graceful it was also good aerodynamically but the flat-fish headlights – seen previously on the Lamborghini Miura – have never been an artistic success.

The 4.5-litre cars were capable of 137-143 mph, depending on whether the rear-mounted gearbox was a manual 5-speeder or an automatic. Road-testers liked the car – it was also chosen as a Car of the Year in 1978 – but the chassis was so good that they wanted more power. This came with the 928S version in 1979; increasing the

SPECIFICATION	PORSCHE 928 GTS
ENGINE	Aluminium V-8 5397 cc
POWER	360 bhp @ 5700 rpm
TRANSMISSION	Manual 5-speed transaxle
CHASSIS	Unitary steel
BRAKES	Discs all round with ABS
TOP SPEED	168 mph (270 km/h)
ACCELERATION	**0-60 mph** 5.4 seconds **0-100 mph** 14.3 seconds

cylinder size brought the capacity to 4.7-litres, the power to 300 bhp and the maximum speed up to 155 mph; there were a few visual changes like the front air-dam and a rear spoiler while lower profile tyres went on wider wheels. Porsche owners still wanted sporting cars.

And the steady increase in power and sophistication has continued ever since. The 1984 S2 had a little more power from the same 4.7-litre to reach 157 mph. Then 1987 saw the 5-litre version with four valves per cylinder giving 320 bhp and 160 mph. By now Porsche had replaced the 2-litre 924 with the 2.5-litre 944, which used, in effect, half the 928's V-8; the 944S was the four-valve version which arrived at the same time as the 928S4 which now had exactly the same bore and stroke as the 944. While the little 924s and 944s had turbo derivatives, the 928 has always used the less stressed alternative.

In 1990, the S4 became the 928GT with 330 bhp, and the final version so far is the GTS, now increased to 5.4-litres and a healthy 350 bhp. On a straight road, it would be a genuine 170 mph car. The 928 was developed at a time when it required faith to invest in big engines, but the continued demand for the car has fully justified that faith and the 928 has become just as much a classic in its own time as the 911.

The 928 was conceived as a full four-seater family GT to replace the 911, but the rear-engined warrior refused to die. The 928 interior is certainly spacious.

Twenty years on and the 1995 928 is some 30 mph faster than the original. Overall lines have changed little.

PORSCHE 911 TURBO

1995
181 mph
(291 km/h)

'Twenty years on the cult is as strong as ever.'

Latest Turbo follows 959 technology with four wheel drive and twin turbochargers to produce massive 408 bhp from 3.6-litres of flat-6.

Any Porsche 911 is a fast car but the Turbo range have been spectacularly fast since the launch of the first one in 1975. While BMW were the first manufacturer to attach a turbocharger to the exhaust system of a production car with the 1973 2002, Porsche arguably gave credence to the cult-following that was to keep growing long after BMW had dropped the idea. Twenty years on the cult is as strong as ever.

Motor racing has always had considerable influence over Porsche's management thinking. The company had enjoyed considerable success with the 917 during the 1969-72 Sports Car Championship until the ruling body killed the formula in favour of thinly disguised 2-seater *Grand Prix* cars. Porsche competition interest then switched to the Stateside Can-Am races where rules were less restrictive; initially open versions of the 917 were used with the 4.5 or 5-litre flat-12 engines of the earlier cars. Seeking even more power, the engineers decided to turbocharge the existing engines rather than develop anything physically bigger; the ultimate version was the 917-30 with the engine increased to 5.4-litres and

turbocharged to produce a phenomenal 1100 bhp – it won the championship in 1973.

Meanwhile the sports car racing rules were set to change again for 1975 to cater for cars that at least looked like road cars (Group 5) and others that were road cars (Group 4). Armed with their recent turbo experience, Porsche began to develop a turbo-charged 911 and were running it during 1974 alongside the open two-seater cars. This was to be the basis of the 935, which carried all before it when the championship finally started in 1976. However, a new car was also needed for the Group 4 category, a customary Porsche preserve; hence a road-going version of the 934 was launched in March 1975 – the Porsche Turbo.

While the racing versions were able to develop over 500 bhp, and last the distance in endurance racing, the production car had a relatively leisurely 260 bhp from its 3-litre engine – enough for a comfortable 155 mph. It still looked like a 911 from the side, but wide tyres with massive wheel arch flares and a big rear wing set the Turbo apart; the wing certainly helped to improve the stability at high speed as it always felt a little nervous when being driven fast. But despite all that power it was very tractable, with so much torque that Porsche only gave it four speeds.

When the 911 SC engine was increased to 3.2-litres in 1977, the Turbo went one better to 3.3-litres

Below: First of the Turbos came in 1975 as the road-going version of the 911 that Porsche wanted to race alongside the 935 and 936. The 911 Turbo might have been the 930, but marketing sense prevailed.

and 300 bhp in European trim, quite a big increase, helped by an intercooler to drop the temperature of the incoming air, and enough to take the maximum speed to 162 mph. While some 1983 revisions gave the engine more torque, the next major change was to wait until 1990, following a temporary cessation of Turbo production while the Carreras 2 and 4 came along. The new version still used a 3.3-litre engine but, with further modifications, the power was raised to 320 bhp; installed in the cleaner Carrera 2 shape, this raised the maximum speed to 167 mph, and a five-speed gearbox helped to lower the 0-60 mph time to a dramatic 4.7 seconds.

Late 1992 saw the arrival of the 3.6-litre version, outwardly unchanged apart from taller wheels, but now with 360 bhp and a 174 mph maximum speed. Vital tenths are difficult to shave from 0-60 mph times whatever the power increase, but particularly with a rear engine adding to the grip; this one recorded 4.6 seconds, but nearly a second off the 0-100 mph time showed that the new-found power was for real.

But at Porsche development never stops. When everyone thought the 911 had reached its peak they launched the Carrera Turbo, a Carrera 4 with twin turbos and 408 bhp, but everyone else just calls it Turbo. In reality it is a refined 959 with even more modern technology and with 4WD and a 6-speed box, it is almost as fast off the mark as

the 959. Thirty years on and the same basic design now handles over three times the power with as much appeal to today's enthusiasts as the original 911 afforded back in 1965.

SPECIFICATION	PORSCHE 911 TURBO (1993)	PORSCHE 911 TURBO (1995)
ENGINE	Turbocharged flat-6 3600 cc	Turbocharged flat-6 3600 cc
HORSEPOWER	360 bhp @ 5500 rpm	408 bhp @ 5750 rpm
TRANSMISSION	Manual 5-speed	Manual 6-speed 4WD
CHASSIS	Unitary steel	Unitary steel
BRAKES	Discs all round with ABS	Discs all round with ABS
TOP SPEED	174 mph (280 km/h)	181 mph (291 km/h)
ACCELERATION	**0-60 mph** 4.6 seconds **0-100 mph** 10.6 seconds	3,7 seconds 9.2 seconds

PORSCHE 911 GT1

1997

190 mph

305 km/h

The roadgoing GT1 closely resembles the sports racer on which it is based. Being 911-related, it is powered by a flat six-cylinder turbocharged engine although mid- rather than rear-located. It produces a formidable 550bhp which is only some 40bhp less than the competition car.

A top speed of over 190 mph and a price tag approaching £600,000 are the mouth watering specifications of the GT1 that Porsche unveiled in April 1997. This exclusive supercar, of which just 30 will be built, is the most potent roadgoing Porsche ever, its mid-located six-cylinder engine developing 544 bhp.

The GT1 project represented an attempt by Porsche to re-establish its dominance of sports racing and, in 1996, came the welcome return of a works entry at Le Mans.

Work on the DM 10 million (£4.2 million) project began at the firm's Weissach technology centre in August 1995 and was completed a record eight months later. The first road test took place there on March 14th 1996, just 14 weeks before the 24-hour race.

Eligible for the Global GT Championship, this series required that the sports racer needed to resemble a road car but, at that stage, the regulations did not specify whether it came before or after the racing version. It is for this reason that the GT1 was superficially akin to a 911 and that the road car appeared some 10 months after its Le Mans debut.

The GT1 is, in essence, the front end and floorpan of a 911, attached to the rear of Porsche's formidable 962 sports racer. This has been dictated by aerodynamic considerations to a great extent because, unlike the 911 that has a rear-mounted, flat-six engine, the 962's is mid-located, thus permitting more slippery body contours.

The bodywork was made from light, but costly, carbon-fibre and Kevlar and the outcome is a shape that is lower and squatter than the 911's although still recognisably related to it.

The car's rear was dominated by a spoiler intended to help keep the 600 bhp generated by the 3.2-litre twin turbocharged, water-cooled, flat-six on the track. Power was conveyed courtesy of a six-speed gearbox.

Two GT1s appeared at Le Mans where they immediately showed their worth and were strongly tipped to win, but placed second and third. There

Left: Close-up of the GT1 road car featured on the Porsche stand at the 1996 British Motor Show. The bodywork is so designed to permit hot air to escape from the front wheels, particularly after the brakes have been applied.

individuals indicated their interest, this was conditional on more power being available.

The factory's response was to take it or leave it, so the potential customers left it . . . Porsche therefore reinstated turbocharging, output shot up to 544bhp and the roadgoing version was back on stream.

A further bonus for using the 911's existing steel hull was that it would not be necessary to crash test a roadgoing version for homologation. With each racing GT1 reputed to have cost around £1 million apiece this is an important consideration.

No motoring magazine has tested a GT1 road car at the time of writing but the factory claims a top speed of over 190 mph, with 62 mph arriving in the blink of an eye, in just 3.7 seconds.

Such astounding acceleration must be allied with impressive braking and the GT1 uses anti lock racing brakes with eight piston calipers at the front and four at the rear. They are backed up by an advanced Bosch anti lock system.

Further refinements include twin catalytic converters, although power steering was a feature of the competition GT1. The two leather-upholstered bucket seats contrast with the single accommodation of the racer.

The car will only be available in left-hand drive form although air conditioning is an optional extra. The interior comes in just one colour: black. However, the customer can specify the body colour of this quicksilver coupé.

'The factory claims a top speed of over 190 mph, with 62 mph arriving in the blink of an eye, in just 3.7 seconds.'

Bare essentials! As befits a model developed from a racer, interior fittings are relatively basic although positively luxurious when compared with the original.

was some compensation for the German make because the race was won by the Porsche-engined TWR Porsche.

Although a single GT1 went on to trounce the McLaren F1 GTRs to win at the four-hour Brands Hatch GT race later in the season, it ceded the championship to the cars from Woking, Surrey. But the factory clearly means business and the menacing GT1s were back in 1997 for their second racing season.

When Porsche announced that it would be producing a roadgoing version of the sports racer, it declared that its output would be detuned by half, to a still respectable but non turbocharged 300 bhp. However, Porsche's project director, Norbert Singer, has said that although 20 to 30

SPECIFICATION	PORSCHE 911 GT1
ENGINE	Turbocharged flat-6, 3200 cc
HORSEPOWER	544 bhp @ 7000 rpm
TRANSMISSION	Manual 6-speed
CHASSIS	Unitary steel
BRAKES	Ventilated disc all round with ABS
TOP SPEED	Over 190 mph (305 km/h)
ACCELERATION	**0-60 mph** 3.7 seconds **0-100 mph** – no figures available

RENAULT ALPINE A610 TURBO

1992

161 mph

(259 km/h)

' It had become a very quick car with a remarkable level of comfort and well developed handling.'

The French challenge to the Porsche 911, the Alpine was for many years the only sporting machine to be produced in a country more concerned with utilitarian transport than exhilarating motoring. Times change and the French market has long had its own share of native sporting hatches, but the Alpine continued to offer fast and comfortable GT 2+2 motoring at a reasonable price; it actually deserved a wider appreciation than it achieved – sadly it ceased production at the end of 1994.

The Alpine has more similarity to the Porsche than just a share of the same market. The layout, with the engine mounted behind the rear axle, is the same and for similar reasons; both trace their origins back to developments of rear engined saloons. Where Porsche eventually made their own engine for the 911, but retained the layout, Alpine have always used Renault engine/gearbox units; the original 1955 A106 used parts from the Renault 750-4CV, and the subsequent A110 shared its drive-train with the R8. When Renault switched to front-wheel-drive, the Renault 16 was the donor for the 1969 Alpine 1600S – a very successful rally machine; a longitudinal engine/gearbox can just as easily be mounted at the back as the front. By now Renault were 30% shareholders and Alpine was Renault's competition department.

Seeking to move up-market Alpine added the A310 in 1971 as a 2+2 using the same running gear under a new distinctive shape. As with its predecessors, the body was a glass-fibre shell mounted on a tubular back-bone frame, but the rear suspension now featured double wishbones rather than the original swing-axles from the earlier Renaults. And it was developed and trimmed to proper GT levels. By the mid-'seventies Renault owned 87% of Alpine whose production now encompassed A110s, A310s and R5 Alpines – the 1975 total was 4500 vehicles; the A110 ceased in 1977.

In 1980, the A310 gained a power unit more appropriate to its GT status with the 2.7-litre Peugeot-Renault-Volvo unit to give a 140 mph top speed. As this was also from a front-wheel-drive Renault – the 30 – the engine was still behind the rear axle. Five years on, the sleeker GTA replaced the A310, with the 160 bhp 2.85-litre V-6 or a 200 bhp 2.5-litre Turbo version, giving just over 150 mph; the chassis design remained the same but the car was longer, lower, wider and heavier as refinement and luxury were added. It had become a very quick car with a remarkable level of comfort and well developed handling.

The final version is the substantially similar A610 Turbo introduced in 1991. The body, still glassfibre, has been widened to accomodate a larger track and the front smoothed with pop-up headlamps. But the biggest change was the use of the 3-litre PRV engine, turbo-charged to produce 250 bhp which propels this low-drag coupé to 161 mph. Alpine has a strong track record, the A610 is a well developed car and was considerably cheaper than a Porsche 911; it should have sold better.

SPECIFICATION	RENAULT ALPINE A610 TURBO
ENGINE	Turbocharged V-6 2975 cc
POWER	250 bhp @ 5750 rpm
TRANSMISSION	Manual 5-speed transaxle
CHASSIS	Steel backbone, g/fibre bodywork
BRAKES	Discs all round with ABS
TOP SPEED	161 mph (259 km/h)
ACCELERATION	**0-60 mph** 5.8 seconds **0-100 mph** 15.8 seconds

The interior had all the luxury trimming expected in a GT; at speed it was a remarkably quiet car.

The French answer to the Porsche 911, the A610 was a fast and effective 2+2 with a glass-fibre body on a steel chassis using turbo-charged Renault power. Despite competition breeding, it was not as popular as it deserved to be.

TVR CERBERA

1996
168 mph
270 km/h

The Griffith is an exhilarating mixture of retro style with modern performance, with an agility that few mid-engined cars can match.

More TVRs emerge from Blackpool in a year than the combined production of Newport Pagnell Aston Martins and Malvern Morgans, but the marque has been far less known outside enthusiast circles than either of those two establishment names. Gradually that is changing; the open TVRs are instantly eye-catching even before the raucous sound of a powerful V-8 turns the heads. And the latest Cerbera 2+2 coupé is just as striking but with TVR's own, more refined, AJP 4.2-litre V-8.

American legislation and litigation deter many small manufacturers and TVR can sell all they want to make elsewhere. So TVRs no longer go to the USA, which is a shame when you look at the origins of the Griffith, the first of the new generation TVRs. Jack Griffith was the American garage-owner who first tried to squeeze a Ford V-8 into the 1600 Mk IIA TVRs that were competing in the 1962 Sebring 12-hour race. From this early attempt came the Griffith 200, a Mark III TVR using a strengthened chassis with the 4.7-litre Ford V-8 installed in either 195 or 271 bhp forms. The Griffith 400 followed in early 1964, the first of the Manx-tailed TVRs. Unfortunately these were not properly developed and affected the TVR reputation; a prolonged US dock-strike hit both companies and bankrupted TVR. Although few Griffiths were sold outside America, the replacement Tuscan V-8, the first of the new Lilley management, was a success and gave over 150 mph in 1967. Tuscan V-6s, Vixens, M-series and Taimars (including the first convertible) took the company through the 'seventies without recapturing that performance level.

The new wedge-shaped Tasmin was the

design for the 'eighties, initially with Ford V-6 power which also temporarily returned the cars to the US market, by which time current owner Peter Wheeler had taken charge from 1981. The Tasmin name was dropped when the Rover unit arrived in 1983 for the 350i convertible. By the mid-'eighties every sports car had to have real performance, so the Rover engine grew to extend the range, providing the 145 mph 390SE and later the 150 mph 420SEAC (Special Edition with Aramid Composite bodywork).

Rover power was used for a special one-make TVR-sponsored Tuscan Challenge for 1989; by the time the 36 race cars were built, TVR had uprated the engines to a dry-sumped re-cranked 4.4-litre developing 350 bhp with four down-draught Weber carburetters, and reworked the chassis to cope with the extra power. The resultant racing was, and still is, a great success, but we had to wait until 1992 for the Griffith, the road-going version of the Tuscan racers.

When the Griffith finally arrived, it had a 4.3-litre Rover unit with 280 bhp installed in a chassis that had learnt the lessons of Tuscan racing, all clad in a curvaceous body that was old and new at the same time, together with an extremely effective quick-action soft-top. The Chimaera followed a year later, a little longer for more luggage space and a little softer for more comfort, with similar lines carrying different detailing. As this was given the option of 4.0 and 4.3-litre units, the Griffith had to move up a league with a 5-litre version

developing a massive 340 bhp; gearing limits the top speed of Rover-powered versions to around 161 mph, but the acceleration of the Griffith 500 is brutally quick with 0-100 mph in just over 10 seconds – and it is less than half the price of a Ferrari 355.

However the Cerbera uses TVR's new overhead camshaft engine which will rev more freely. A little more power and better aerodynamics will lift the maximum speed towards 170 mph, although the initial acceleration will be less dramatic due to the extra weight of a 2+2 coupé. With an extra 11 inches in the wheelbase the new family TVR should considerably broaden the marque's appeal.

Above and left: A permanent hard-top plus an extra 11 inches in the wheelbase make the Cerbera into a reasonable family coupé.

'The Cerbera uses TVR's new overhead camshaft engine which will rev more freely.'

SPECIFICATION	TVR CERBERA
ENGINE	Aluminium V-8, 4185 cc
HORSEPOWER	360 bhp @ 6500 rpm
TRANSMISSION	Manual 5-speed
CHASSIS	Tubular frame, grp body
BRAKES	Discs all round
TOP SPEED	168 mph (270 km/h)
ACCELERATION	**0-60 mph** 4.5 seconds **0-100 mph** 9.9 seconds

VAUXHALL LOTUS CARLTON

1990

173 mph

278 km/h

The Lotus Carlton is such an unlikely car. Derived from Vauxhall's top of the range saloon, normally a fast and comfortable 5-seater with few sporting pretensions, it is a product of General Motors' 1986-94 ownership of the Norfolk sports car specialist. GM had bought Lotus for Lotus Engineering rather than the low-volume production side and the Lotus Carlton was as much a flag-ship for engineering ability as for the Vauxhall range. Despite its GM parentage, Lotus Engineering was a facility that also worked for other manufacturers once they were convinced that GM did not have access to the confidential files; the Lotus Carlton was a demonstration of what could be done – it was also sold as the Opel Lotus Omega.

At the time of its June 1990 production start, the 173 mph Lotus Carlton cost £48,000 while the 146 mph 3.0 GSi 24-valve Carlton from which it came was a mere £25,635.

It was a Vauxhall which went straight into top BMW and Mercedes territory and out-performed them all – the subsequent BMW M5 6-speed was its nearest equivalent – but for all its

performance it was still a Vauxhall or an Opel and never had the cachet required for that end of the market. It ran for just over two years.

The basic Carlton 3.0 GSi 24-valve engine develops a useful 204 bhp at 6000 rpm using twin overhead camshafts and Bosch fuel injection. Lotus squeezed the maximum out of the 6-cylinder block by a small overbore but made a new crankshaft to increase the capacity from 2969 to 3638 cc; to this were added a pair of Garrett T25 turbochargers to give 10 psi pressure – two small turbos give less turbo-lag than a single larger one – with Rochester (from GM US) fuel injection. The result was 377 bhp at 5200 rpm with torque (mid-range pulling power) more than doubled. All this required a new, stronger gearbox which came from ZF as a 6-speeder with a very high top gear ratio to give 70 mph at just 1650 rpm.

Such a performance increase obviously demanded chassis improvements to be safe; the brakes use ventilated discs with four-pot calipers at the front and the new alloy wheels are taller with low profile tyres and wider, increasing the track at both ends.

Twin turbochargers and an extra 670 cc capacity help to increase 24-valve Carlton power from 204 to 377 bhp.

Big alloy wheels, revised front end and rear wing give a distinctive appearance to the Lotus version.

The standard system of independent suspension is retained, but stiffened and strengthened, while the rear suspension features variable rate coils and self-levelling suspension to ensure that the car remains at the right height for the aerodynamics to work effectively however much weight is being carried – the front spoiler and the rear wing combine to create zero lift, while the drag factor is an impressive 0.307.

While the basic bodyshell comes from the standard Carlton, it looks quite different with the spoiler, side skirts and rear wing; it has the distinction of being the world's fastest ever production 5-seater. Although the model was not a success, lessons have certainly been absorbed within GM. In fact, some of its design stemmed from the work that Lotus did for GM in the development of the Corvette ZR-1 which was the first to use that ZF 6-speed gearbox coupled to a Lotus-designed 32-valve V-8 engine; the standard Corvette uses the same 6-speed gearbox mated to a normal GM 16-valve 5.7-litre V-8, a combination that is now used in the faster of GM's other sporting cars, the Chevrolet Camaro Z-28 and the Pontiac Firebird Trans-Am. With 277 bhp, the latter clocks 158 mph and can reach 100 mph in 16 seconds – it goes as well as it looks. The Lotus Carlton is the ultimate wolf in sheep's clothing.

'The Lotus Carlton is the ultimate wolf in sheep's clothing.'

SPECIFICATION	VAUXHALL LOTUS CARLTON
ENGINE	Turbo straight-6, 3638 cc
HORSEPOWER	377 bhp @ 5200 rpm
TRANSMISSION	Manual 6-speed
CHASSIS	Unitary steel
BRAKES	Discs all round with ABS
TOP SPEED	173 mph
ACCELERATION	**0-60 mph** 5.3 seconds **0-100 mph** 10.9 seconds

Is this the fastest five-seater? At 173 mph this is a shade faster than BMW's latest M5.

VENTURI 400GT

1995
175 mph
281 km/h

'It is impressively fast – stable too – and will reach 180 mph.'

When such revered names as Delage, Delahaye, Bugatti, Talbot died in the wake of post-war luxury taxes, France cut off its performance heritage. Since then, the Ligier road cars have come and gone, Renault with Alpine persevered until the A610, too, has ceased, and it is now left to the little firm of Venturi to resuscitate a tradition of French sporting machinery that stretches back to the beginning of motor racing.

Founded in 1984 by two racing enthusiasts, Claude Poiraud and Gerard Godfroy, Venturi showed its first prototype later that year; the Paris Show in 1986 saw the official launch of the first of the high quality mid-engined sports cars that are now assembled in Nantes. Turbo-charged V-6 engines and transmissions came from Renault, but, unlike the Alpine, these were mounted amidships rather than behind the rear axle, and the power outputs were higher with more turbo boost pressure. For the chassis they used a full length pressed steel frame well boxed for stiffness; wishbone suspension is used at the front while the rear has upper and lower radius arms with transverse links, single at the top and a parallel pair below, following racing practice.

This is all covered by composite bodywork of a striking, yet simple, shape with built-in downforce and a low drag factor of 0.31. Inside it is trimmed with all the care that goes into an Aston Martin with taut leather and polished wood veneers, and there is air-conditioning too. The first one, now the 210, used the 2.5-litre V-6 with a single Garrett T3 turbocharger working to 0.85 bar pressure for 210 bhp to give a maximum speed around 152 mph; the comparable Renault 25 installation produced 182 bhp. The 260 with the 2.85-litre V-6 received similar treatment and 1 bar of boost pressure to give 260 bhp and a maximum of 165 mph; the 260 comes in normal 1255 Kg form and as the lightened Atlantique at 1110 Kg dispensing with such heavyweight luxuries as air conditioning, electric seat adjustment and radio/cassette system in the quest for faster acceleration.

Both 210 and 260 are offered in coupé and 'Transcoupé' form. The latter is an ingenious convertible; you can have *coupe de ville* motoring by removing one or both of the two roof panels, or go one stage further for full open motoring by pressing a button to hinge the rear window/roll-bar assembly forward so that it lies flush with the

With PRV V-6 engines mounted amidships the Venturis are neat and effective machines, ranging from the 2.5-litre 210 to the twin-turbo 3-litre 400GT; shown is the intermediate 300.

rear deck – a true convertible. When up, it is a notchback coupé without the little rear wing that sits across the tail on the coupés.

As part of the promotion of the new Venturis, a one-make race series was organised from 1992 as a support race to major International events; called the Gentleman Drivers Trophy, it was for enthusiastic but skilled amateurs who would pay to race factory-prepared identical cars. For this Venturi produced the 400, using twin turbos on the 3-litre V-6 to generate 408 bhp and special dog-clutch close ratios within the standard casing; the chassis was widened and lengthened to accept the bigger power pack, increase high speed stability and provide higher cornering power. The body grew an integrated

SPECIFICATION	VENTURI 400GT
ENGINE	Aluminium V-6 twin-turbo 2975 cc
HORSEPOWER	408 bhp @ 6000 rpm
TRANSMISSION	Manual 5-speed
CHASSIS	Steel chassis, composite body
BRAKES	Discs all round
TOP SPEED	175 mph
ACCELERATION	**0-60 mph** 4.7 seconds **0-100 mph** 10.4 seconds

Ferrari F40-style rear wing and was 11 inches wider to accommodate a wider track and wider tyres and provide side scoops for engine air and brake cooling; the nose was shorter and blunter with the previous pop-up headlights now partially exposed. They were successful racers for the two seasons, so a road version was produced as the 400GT reverting to the road-going synchromesh gearbox; with 408 bhp in 1150 Kg it is impressively fast – stable too – and will reach nearly 180 mph.

Some of the 400's features have now been carried across to the tamer Atlantique 300, which uses the 3-litre engine and a single turbo to generate 270 bhp; this has the longer wheelbase but narrower rear tyres than the 400, so that it is only 5.5 inches wider than the 210/260; the extra width slows it down so the maximum is similar to that of the 260.

Few testers have sampled the Venturis, so the figures above are conservatively approximate based on calculations and the few reports that have appeared. They won't be far out and show that the Venturi 400GT is a serious supercar, compact and effective.

The 400GT is the road-going development of the cars used for the Gentleman Racer series; with 408 bhp in 1150 Kg it is very fast.

Venturi in its simplest body style is shown with this 260 with no extra rear intakes, no wheel-arch flares.

THEY HAVE ALSO RUN . . .

We close with a handful of cars for which full independent performance figures have not been taken. They have all been, or are still, in limited volume production – they are all fast and deserve a place in any book on fast cars.

Isdera Imperator 108i
top speed 176 mph

Eberhard Schulz, an engineer with Porsche's external research and development facility, established Isdera (an acronym for *Ingenuieuboro fur Styling, Design and Racing*) in Stuttgart in 1981. As an advertisement for his abilities, he built the mid-engined Spyder (open) 033i with spaceframe chassis. A 2.3-litre, four-cylinder engine by Mercedes-Benz was employed, a make that then powered all subsequent Isderas.

When the inevitable requests came for replicas, Schulz obliged and also produced the supplementary 036i 3-litre six.

This was followed in 1984 by the Imperator 108i gull-wing coupé on similar lines but using the 5.8-litre V-8. Based on a 1978 Mercedes-Benz design with which Schulz had been involved,

The Stuttgart-built exclusive mid-engined Isdera Imperator 108i coupé of 1987, based on Mercedes-Benz design study CW311. The two cars are outwardly very similar, even down to roof-mounted rear view mirror!

the 176 mph car was able to reach 60 mph in 5 seconds and 100 mph in 10.8 seconds.

Later, in 1993, came the 112i Commendatore, a coupé named in tribute to Enzo Ferrari that cost the equivalent of £350,000. The well appointed car was powered by the 6-litre V-12 engine used in the top line S-Class Mercedes saloons. There was an alternative 6.9-litre unit with a claimed top speed of 230 mph and a 0-62 mph time of 4.1 seconds.

Spectre R42
estimated top speed 176 mph

An all-new mid-engined luxury supercar, the Spectre R42 was the product of Poole-based GT Developments, who produced over 330 GT40 replicas in the last ten years. The R42 embodied all that experience into newer technology; it uses an aluminium honeycomb chassis with steel sub-frames, the rear one carrying a 350 bhp version of the 4.6-litre 4-cam 32-valve Ford V-8, mated to their own 5-speed transaxle. Carbon-glass-fibre composites are used for the body which is styled very much as a road-going sports racer. Low drag

and light weight ensure that it is very quick. And it is comfortable, too, with well padded leather interior, good sound deadening and enough suspension compliance to keep road noise down and ride comfort up.

In the final phase of prototype development, GTD was taken over by Spectre Motor Car Inc., a US company quoted on the NASDQ bulletin board. The R42 is substantially the same as the GTD version but power steering has been added. It is now in production and over 20 have been completed. Racing versions – GTRs – will be available for the International GT events and the company plans to race its own car in 1997.

Vector W8
estimated top speed 200 mph

Founded in 1978, Vector produced a handful of exotic hi-tech performance cars before the W8 arrived in 1990 – at least 22 were built. These have a carbon-fibre monocoque, gull-wing doors in a composite body with a transverse mid-mounted twin-turbo 634 bhp Corvette 6-litre V-8 mated to a GM 3-speed automatic transmission. The earlier, similar W2 used an aluminium honeycomb chassis, as does the more modern-looking WX3, shown at Geneva in 1993. The

company was taken over by MegaTech in 1994 and should benefit from some Lamborghini input but was in trouble again at the end of 1996.

Monteverdi Hai 650F1
estimated top speed 190 mph

Peter Monteverdi began making high performance GTs in Switzerland in 1967 using a big Chrysler 7-litre in a steel frame de Dion-axled chassis with elegant Fissore bodywork. The 375S and 400SS were joined by the 375L 2+2 using a similar body style. In 1971, he introduced the mid-engined Hai 450SS using the powerful Chrysler 7-litre Hemi in a Fiore-styled Fissore body; only a few were made. Other models included the hemi-powered Berlinetta and the Palm Beach convertible. To celebrate 40 years since the first Monteverdi, 1992 saw the Hai 650 F1 of which four have been built; carbon fibre is used for chassis and bodywork with 650 bhp supplied by a Cosworth DFR 3.5-litre F1 power unit – a road-going *Grand Prix* car.

Ascari FGT
estimated top speed 175 mph

A racing version of the new Ascari FGT appeared in the April 1995 Le Mans pre-qualifying event, but a gearbox problem intervened. However honour was satisfied in the late season Le Mans 4-hours when the car finished third and

another won the final National GT race at Silverstone. The design is that of Lee Noble who has produced racing GT cars for the UK Prosport 3000 series, and the Ultima, two of which were used as mechanical mules for McLaren F1 development. Noble's partner in Ascari Cars Ltd is Klaas Zwart, a businessman racing driver.

The construction is traditional, with a tubular space-frame boxed by aluminium panels bonded and rivetted into place under a well finished and attractive grp body. While the racing versions have used the big 5.7-litre pushrod Ford V-8, road cars will now use the BMW 4-litre V-8 with around 325 bhp instead of the planned Ford quad-cam; this will be mated to a Porsche 6-speed gearbox. The plan is to produce 50 cars a year, some of which will be track cars.

Left: A 1996 Spectre R42. The firm's new owners, headed by Swedish entrepreneur Olaf Hildebrand, are planning to market an improved version. The intention is that output will reach 200 units by 1998.

The race bred mid-engined Ascari GT of 1995. As this is the road going version, a BMW V-8 engine was employed. Otherwise the theme is conventional with the good looking glass-reinforced-plastic coupé body.

Left: The Los Angeles-built Vector W2, introduced in 1980, powered by a 5.8-litre twin turbocharged Chevrolet V-8 engine with a special alloy block and drive taken through a reversed Oldsmobile Toronado transmission.

Fastest Cars Database

Model	Year	Max speed	0-60 mph	0-100 mph
McLaren F1	1993	231	3.2	6.3
McLaren F1 LM	1995	220	3.0	5.9
Bugatti EB110S	1994	218	4.3	9.2
Jaguar XJ220	1993	217	3.6	7.9
Bugatti EB110 GT	1994	212	4.5	9.6
Lamborghini Diablo SE30	1995	207	4.2	9.3
Lamborghini Diablo	1991	205	4.4	9.7
Ferrari F50	1995	202	3.9	7.2
Lamborghini Diablo VT	1994	202	4.9	10.3
Lister Storm GTL	1997	200	4.0	8.0
Ferrari 550 Maranello	1996	199	4.6	10.1
Ferrari F40	1992	198	4.1	7.6
Porsche 959	1986	197	3.7	8.5
Ferrari F512M	1995	191	4.8	10.2
Porsche GT1	1997	190	3.7	–
Lamborghini Countach QV5000S	1986	190	4.9	11.0
Ferrari 288GTO	1986	189	5.0	11.0
Ferrari 512 TR	1992	188	5.0	10.2
Chrysler Viper Venom	1995	187	4.4	9.7
Ferrari 456GT	1994	187	5.1	11.6
Aston Martin Vantage Zagato	1986	186	4.8	11.3
Aston Martin Vantage	1993	184	4.6	10.1
Ferrari Testa Rossa	1985	182	5.7	11.9
Porsche 911 Carrera Turbo3.6	1995	181	3.7	9.2
Venturi 400GT	1995	180	4.7	10.4
Ferrari F355	1994	178	4.6	10.6
Isdera Imperator 108i	1987	176	5.0	10.8
Lamborghini Countach	1975	175	5.6	13.1
Ferrari 365GTB4 Daytona	1971	174	5.4	12.6
Porsche 911 Turbo 3.6	1993	174	4.6	10.6
Vauxhall Lotus Carlton	1990	173	5.3	10.9
Ferrari 365GT4BB	1975	172	6.5	13.5
Lamborghini Miura P400S	1970	172	6.7	15.1
Lotus Esprit V-8	1996	172	4.5	11.3
Aston Martin Vantage	1977	170	5.4	13.0
BMW 850CSi	1994	170	6.5	15.4
BMW M5 6-sp	1994	170	5.4	13.6
Chevrolet Corvette	1996	170	4.7	11.0
Marcos Mantis	1996	170	4.1	–
Porsche 928S4 GTS 5.4	1992	168	5.4	14.3
TVR Cerbera	1996	168	4.5	9.9
Chrysler Viper	1993	167	4.6	10.7
Porsche 911 Turbo 3.3	1991	167	4.7	11.4
Ferrari 250GTO	1963	165	6.1	12.6
Ferrari 410 Superamerica	1959	165	6.6	14.5
Porsche 928 GT	1991	165	5.6	13.4
Venturi 260	1994	165	5.5	14.8
Ford GT40 Mk III	1966	164	5.3	11.8
Ferrari 348 tb	1990	163	5.6	13.3
Ferrari 348GTS	1994	163	5.9	13.9
Ferrari 512BB	1978	163	6.2	13.6
Porsche 928 S4 5.0	1988	163	5.3	12.7
Renault Alpine A610	1992	163	5.9	15.8
BMW M1	1979	162	5.4	13.5
BMW M3	1993	162	5.4	13.1
Jaguar D 3.4	1956	162	4.7	12.1
Marcos LM 500	1995	162	4.6	11.9
Monteverdi Hai 450SS	1970	162	5.0	11.8
Aston Martin DB7	1994	161	5.8	14.4
Iso Grifo A3L	1966	161	7.4	16.6
Lotus Sport 300	1993	161	4.7	11.7
TVR Griffith 4.3	1992	161	4.7	11.1
TVR Griffith 500	1993	161	4.2	10.3
AC Cobra 427	1965	160	4.6	10.1
Aston Martin DBS V-8	1971	160	5.9	13.8
Audi RS2 Estate	1994	160	4.8	13.1
Chevrolet Corvette 427	1968	160	6.3	14.3
De Tomaso Pantera GT5-S	1986	160	5.4	13.1
Honda NSX	1994	160	5.3	12.6
Lotus Esprit S4	1993	160	5.0	12.7
Maserati Bora	1973	160	6.5	14.7
Maserati Shamal	1994	160	5.4	13.0
Porsche Carrera 3.6	1994	160	5.2	12.9
BMW 850i	1991	159	7.1	17.3
Ferrari 275 GTB4	1966	159	6.4	12.5
Honda NSX	1990	159	5.8	13.7
Lotus Esprit Turbo SE	1989	159	4.9	12.4
Mercedes 600SEL (A)	1991	159	6.7	15.8
Mercedes 600SL (A)	1992	159	6.0	14.4
Porsche 911 Cabrio	1994	159	5.0	12.3
Chevrolet Corvette 5.7	1993	158	5.5	14.3
Ferrari 412	1986	158	6.5	15.2
Jaguar XK-8	1996	158	6.2	16.1
Lamborghini Urraco P300	1975	158	7.6	17.5
Maserati Khamsin	1978	158	6.5	16.8
Pontiac Firebird Trans-Am 5.7	1992	158	6.3	16.2
Porsche 928 S2 4.7	1984	158	6.2	15.8
Porsche Carrera 2	1989	158	5.1	12.7
TVR Chimaera 4.0	1993	158	5.2	13.2
Aston Martin Virage	1990	157	6.8	15.5
BMW M5	1990	157	6.4	15.6
Ferrari 308 GTB QV	1983	157	5.7	14.3
Jaguar XJR-S 6.0	1991	157	7.0	16.4
Lamborghini Islero 400GTS	1969	157	5.9	13.7
Lamborghini Jarama	1971	157	6.8	16.4
Mercedes 500 SL (A)	1989	157	5.9	14.0
Lamborghini 400 GT	1966	156	7.0	17.1
Maserati Indy 4.7	1971	156	7.7	17.6
Mazda RX-7	1992	156	6.0	15.8
Mercedes 500E	1991	156	6.3	14.7
Nissan 300ZX	1990	156	5.6	14.5
Porsche Carrera 4	1989	156	5.2	14.0
Toyota Supra 3.0	1993	156	5.1	12.3
Aston Martin V-8	1973	155	5.7	13.6
Audi A8 4.2 Quattro	1994	155	8.3	19.1
Bentley Continental S	1994	155	5.5	17.2
BMW 740i (A)	1994	155	8.8	21.2
BMW 750iL (A)	1987	155	7.7	17.8
BMW M3 Cabrio	1994	155	5.7	14.3
Ferrari 250GT	1960	155	6.5	12.8
Jaguar XJR-S 6.0	1992	155	6.3	15.1
Jaguar XJS	1976	155	6.7	16.2
Lexus LS400	1995	155	8.5	20.8
Mercedes 500SE (A)	1993	155	6.8	17.2
Porsche 911 Turbo 3.0	1975	155	6.0	13.2
TVR Tuscan SE	1966	155	5.7	13.8
Ferrari 308 GT4	1976	154	6.9	18.1
Ferrari 308 GTB	1976	154	6.8	16.5
Ferrari Mondial t	1991	154	5.6	13.9
Ford Sierra RS500	1987	154	6.1	16.2
Monteverdi 375S	1970	154	7.2	15.5
Porsche 911 Carrera 3.2	1987	154	5.6	14.0
Renault Alpine GTA Turbo	1986	154	6.0	16.3
Bentley Continental R	1991	153	6.2	18.5
Ferrari 328 GTB	1987	153	5.5	13.8
Ferrari 400i	1985	153	6.7	15.6
Jaguar XJR	1994	153	5.7	15.1
Lamborghini Espada	1972	153	7.8	18.1
Maserati Ghibli	1994	153	5.6	13.6
Mercedes S500 Coupé (A)	1994	153	7.9	20.2
Mitsubishi 3000GT	1992	153	5.8	16.1
Porsche 911 Carrera RS 2.7	1973	153	5.5	15.0
Porsche 968	1992	153	6.1	15.7
Aston Martin DB4GT Zagato	1962	152	6.1	14.1
Aston Martin DB6	1966	152	6.0	14.9
BMW 750i (A)	1989	152	7.3	17.0
Chevrolet Corvette 427	1966	152	5.4	12.8
Chevrolet Corvette 427	1971	152	5.3	12.7
Jaguar XJS HE	1982	152	6.5	17.8
Porsche 944 Turbo SE	1988	152	5.7	14.2
Venturi 210	1987	152	6.7	17.9
Chevrolet Corvette 5.7	1985	151	6.0	16.5
Ferrari 365 GTC	1969	151	6.3	14.7
Porsche 928S 4.5 (A)	1985	151	6.7	17.3
BMW M635 CSi	1989	150	6.0	15.1
Ferrari 365GT4 2+2	1975	150	7.1	18.0
Ferrari 400GT (A)	1979	150	8.0	18.7
Jaguar E 3.8 fhc	1961	150	6.9	16.2
Jaguar E 4.2 fhc	1964	150	7.0	17.2
Lamborghini 350GT	1964	150	6.4	16.3
Lotus Esprit Turbo	1988	150	5.4	13.3
Porsche 911 SC	1983	150	5.4	14.8
Porsche 911S 2.4	1972	150	6.2	17.1
TVR 420 SEAC	1988	150	4.7	12.3
Vauxhall Calibra 2.0 Turbo	1992	150	6.2	16.9